The Voyage of
H.M.S. Pandora

'H. M. S. *Pandora* in the act of foundering'

The Voyage of H.M.S. Pandora

In Pursuit of the Mutineers of
the *Bounty* in the South Seas
1790–1791

Edward Edwards R. N.
the Commander of the *Pandora*

George Hamilton
the Surgeon of the *Pandora*

edited by
Basil Thomson

LEONAUR

*The Voyage of H.M.S. Pandora: in Pursuit of the Mutineers of
the Bounty in the South Seas—1790-1791*
by Edward Edwards R. N. & George Hamilton
edited by Basil Thomson

Leonaur an imprint of Oakpast Ltd

ISBN: 978-1-84677-602-1 (hardcover)
ISBN: 978-1-84677-601-4 (softcover)

http://www.leonaur.com

Publisher's Notes

The opinions expressed in this book are those of the author
and are not necessarily those of the publisher.

Contents

Introduction

None of the minor incidents in our naval history has inspired so many writers as the mutiny of the *Bounty*. Histories, biographies and romances, from Bligh's narrative in 1790 to Mr. Becke's *Mutineers* in 1898, have been founded upon it; Byron took it for the theme of the least happy of his dramatic poems; and all these, not because the mutiny left any mark upon history, but because it ranks first among the stories of the sea, instinct with the living elements of romance, of primal passion and of tragedy—all moving to a happy ending in the Arcadia of Pitcairn Island. And yet, while every incident in the moving story, even to the evidence in the famous court-martial, has been discussed over and over again, there has been lying in the Record Office for more than a century an autograph manuscript, written by one of the principal actors in the drama, which no one has thought it worth while to print.

Though the story of the mutiny is too well known to need repeating in detail, it is necessary to set forth as briefly as possible its relation to the history of maritime discovery in the Pacific. In the year 1787, ten years after the death of Captain Cook in Hawaii, a number of West India merchants in London, stirred by the glowing reports of the natural wealth of the South Sea Islands brought home by Dampier and Cook, petitioned the government to acclimatize the bread-fruit in Jamaica. A ship of 215 tons was purchased into the service and fitted out under the direct superintendence of Sir Joseph Banks, who named her the *Bounty*, and recommended William Bligh, one of Cook's officers, for the command. It was a new departure. The object of most of the earlier government expeditions to the South Seas had been the advancement of geographical science and natural history; the voyage of the *Bounty* was to turn former discoveries to the profit of the empire.

Bligh was singularly ill-fitted for the command. While he had undoubted ability, his whole career shows him to have been wanting in the tact and temper without which no one can successfully lead men; and in this venture his own defects were aggravated by the inefficiency of his officers. He took in his cargo of bread-fruit trees at Tahiti, and there was no active insubordination until he reached Tonga on the homeward voyage. At sunrise on April 28th, 1789, the crew mutinied under the leadership of Fletcher Christian, the Master's Mate, whom Bligh's ungoverned temper had provoked beyond endurance. The seamen had other motives. Bligh had kept them far too long at Tahiti, and during the five months they had spent at the island, every man had formed a connection among the native women, and had enjoyed a kind of life that contrasted sharply with the lot of blue-jackets a century ago. Forcing Bligh, and such of their shipmates as were loyal to him, into the launch, and casting them adrift with food and water barely sufficient for a week's subsistence, they set the ship's course eastward, crying "Huzza for Tahiti!" There followed an open boat voyage that is unexampled in maritime history. The boat was only 23 feet long; the weight of eighteen men sank her almost to the gunwale; the ocean before them was unknown, and teeming with hidden dangers; their only arms against hostile natives were a few cutlasses, their only food two ounces of biscuit each a day; and yet they ran 3618 nautical miles in forty-one days, and reached Timor with the loss of only one man, and he was killed by the natives at the very outset.

The mutineers fared as mutineers have always fared. Having sailed the ship to Tahiti, they fell out among themselves, half taking the *Bounty* to the uninhabited island of Pitcairn, where they were discovered twenty-seven years later, and half remaining at Tahiti. Of these two were murdered, four were drowned in the wreck of the *Pandora*, three were hanged in England, and six were pardoned, one living to become a post-captain in the navy, another to be gunner on the *Blenheim* when she foundered with Sir Thomas Troubridge.

One boat voyage only is recorded as being longer than Bligh's. In 1536 Diego Botelho Pereira made the passage from Portuguese India to Lisbon in a native *fusta*, or lateen rigged boat, but a little larger than Bligh's. He had, however, covered her with a deck, and provisioned her for the venture, and he was able to replenish his stock at various points on the voyage.

In 1790 the publication of Bligh's account of his sufferings excited the strongest public sympathy, and the Admiralty lost no time in fitting out an expedition to search for the mutineers, and bring them home to punishment. The *Pandora*, frigate, of 24 guns, was commissioned for the purpose, and manned by 160 men, composed largely of landsmen, for every trained seaman in the navy had gone to man the great fleet then assembling at Portsmouth under Lord Howe. Captain Edward Edwards, the officer chosen for the command, had a high reputation as a seaman and a disciplinarian, and from the point of view of the Admiralty, who intended the cruise simply as a police mission without any scientific object, no better choice could have been made. Their orders to him were to proceed to Tahiti, and, not finding the mutineers there, to visit the different groups of the Society and Friendly Islands, and the others in the neighbouring parts of the Pacific, using his best endeavours to seize and bring home in confinement the whole, or such part of the delinquents as he might be able to discover. The orders ran:

> You are to keep the mutineers as closely confined as may preclude all possibility of their escaping, having, however, proper regard to the preservation of their lives, that they may be brought home to undergo the punishment due to their demerits.

Edwards belonged to that useful class of public servant that lives upon instructions. With a roving commission in an ocean studded with undiscovered islands the possibilities of scientific discovery were immense, but he faced them like a blinkered horse that has his eyes fixed on the narrow track before him, and all the pleasant byways of the road shut out. A cold, hard man, devoid of sympathy and imagination, of every interest beyond the straitened limits of his profession, Edwards in the eye of posterity was almost the worst man that could have been chosen. For, with a different commander, the voyage would have been one of the most important in the history of South Sea discovery, and the account he has written of it compares in style and colour with a log-book.

In Edwards' place a more genial man, a Catoira, a Wallis, or a Cook, would have written a journal of discovery that might have taken a place in the front rank of the literature of travel. He would have investigated the murder of La Pérouse's boat's crew in Tutuila on the spot; he would have rescued the survivors of that ill-fated expedition whose smoke-signals he saw on Vanikoro; he would have brought home news of the great Fiji group through which Bligh passed in the *Bounty*'s launch; he might even have discovered Fletcher Christian's colony of mutineers in Pitcairn. But, on the other hand, humanity to his prisoners might have furnished them with the means of escape, and his ardour for discovery might have led him into dangers from which no one would have survived to tell the tale. Edwards had the qualities of his defects. If he treated his prisoners harshly, he prevented them from contaminating his crew, and brought the majority of them home alive through all the perils of shipwreck and famine. In all the attacks that have been made upon him there is not a word against his character as a plain, straightforward officer, who could lick a crew of landsmen into shape, and keep them loyal to him through the stress of shipwreck and privation. If he was callous to the sufferings of his prisoners, he was at least as indifferent to his own. If he felt no sympathy with others, he asked for none with himself. If he won no love, he compelled respect.

Of his officers little need be said. Corner, the first lieutenant, was a stout seaman, who bottled up his disapproval of his captain's behaviour until the commission was out. Hayward, the second lieutenant, was a time-server. He had been a midshipman on the *Bounty* at the time of the mutiny, and an intimate friend of young Peter Heywood who was constrained to cast in his lot with the mutineers, yet, when Heywood gave himself up on the arrival of the *Pandora* at Tahiti, his old comrade, now risen in the world, received him with a haughty stare. Of Larkin, Passmore, and the rest, we know nothing.

Fortunately for us, the *Pandora* carried a certain rollicking, irresponsible person as surgeon. George Hamilton has been called:

. . . . a coarse, vulgar, and illiterate man, more disposed to relate licentious scenes and adventures, in which he and his companions were engaged, than to give any information of proceedings and occurrences connected with the main object of the voyage.

From this puritanical criticism most readers will dissent. Hamilton was bred in Northumberland, and was at this time past forty. His portrait, the frontispiece to his book, represents him in the laced coat and powdered wig of the period, a man of middle age, with clever, well-cut features, and a large, humorous, and rather sensual mouth. His book, with all its faults of scandalous plain speech, is one that few naval surgeons of that day could have written. The style, though flippant, is remarkable for a cynical but always good-natured humour, and on the rare occasions when he thought it professionally incumbent on him to be serious, as in his discussion of the best dietary for long voyages, and the physical effects of privations, his remarks display observation and good sense. It must be admitted, I fear, that he relates certain of his own and his shipmates' adventures ashore with shameless gusto, but he wrote in an age that loved plain speech, and that did not care to veil its appetite for licence. Like Edwards, he tells us little of the prisoners after they were consigned to "Pandora's Box." His narrative is valuable as a commentary on Edwards' somewhat meagre report, and for the sidelights which it throws upon the manners of naval officers of those days. Even Edwards, to whom he is always loyal, does not escape his little shaft of satire when he relates how the stern captain was driven to conduct prayers in the most desperate portion of the boat voyage. His book, published at Berwick in 1793, has now become so rare that Mr. Quaritch lately advertised for it three times without success, and therefore no excuse is needed for reprinting it.

The *Pandora* was dogged by ill luck from the first. An epidemic fever raging in England at the time of her departure, was introduced on board, it was thought, by infected clothing. The sick bay, and indeed, the officers' cabins, too, were crammed with stores intended for the return voyage of the *Bounty*, and there was no accommodation for the sick. Hamilton attributes their recovery to the use of tea and sugar, then carried for the first time in a ship of war. He gives some interesting information regarding the precautions taken against scurvy. They had essence of malt and hops for brewing beer, a mill for grinding wheat, the meal being eaten with brown sugar, and as much *sauerkraut* as the crew chose to eat.

The first land sighted after rounding Cape Horn, was Ducie's island; probably the same island which, as the Encarnacion of Quiros, has dodged about the charts of the old geographers, swelling into a continent, contracting into an atoll, and finally coming to rest in the neighbourhood of the Solomon Islands before vanishing for ever. The *Pandora* was now in the latitude of Pitcairn, which lay down wind only three hundred miles distant. If she had but kept a westerly course, she must have sighted it, for the island's peak is visible for many leagues, but relentless ill fortune turned her northward, and during the ensuing day she passed the men she was in search of scarce thirty leagues away. One glimmer of good fortune awaited Edwards in Tahiti. The schooner built by the mutineers was ready for sea, but not provisioned for a voyage. She put to sea, and outsailed the *Pandora's* boat that went in chase of her, but her crew, dreading the inevitable starvation that faced them, put back during the night and took to the mountains, where they were all captured.

In the matter of "Pandora's Box," there were excuses for Edwards, who was bitterly attacked afterwards for his inhumanity. One of the chiefs had warned him that there was a plot between the natives and the mutineers to cut the cable of the *Pandora* in the night. Most of the mutineers were connected through their women with influential chiefs, and nothing was more likely than that such a rescue should be attempted. His own crew, moreover, were human. They could see for themselves the charms of a life in Tahiti; they could hear from the prisoners the consideration in which Englishmen were held in this delightful land. What had been possible in the *Bounty* was possible in the *Pandora*. Edwards regarded his prisoners as pirates, desperate with the weight of the rope about their necks. His orders were definite—to consider nothing but the preservation of their lives—and he did his duty in his own way according to his lights. And that he was not insensible to every feeling of humanity is shown by the fact that he allowed the native wives of the mutineers daily access to their husbands while the ship lay there. The infinitely pathetic story of poor Peggy, the beautiful Tahitian girl who had borne a child to midshipman Stewart, was vouched for six years later by the missionaries of the Duff. She had to be separated from her husband by force, and it was at his request that she was not again admitted to the ship. Poor girl! it was all her life to her. A month before her boy-husband perished in the wreck of the *Pandora*, she had died of a broken heart, leaving her baby, the first half-caste born in Tahiti, to be brought up by the missionaries.

"Pandora's Box" certainly needed some excuse. A round house, eleven feet long, accessible only through a scuttle in the roof, was built upon the quarter deck as a prison for the fourteen mutineers, who were ironed and handcuffed. Hamilton says that the roundhouse was built partly out of consideration for the prisoners themselves, in order to spare them the horrors of prolonged imprisonment below in the tropics, and that although the service regulations restricted prisoners to two-thirds allowance, Edwards rationed them exactly like the ship's company. Morrison, however, who seems to have belonged to that objectionable class of seamen—the sea-lawyer—having kept a journal of grievances against Bligh when on the *Bounty*, and preserved it even in "Pandora's Box," gives a very different account, and Peter Heywood, a far more trustworthy witness, declared in a letter to his mother, that they were kept "with both hands and both legs in irons, and were obliged to eat, drink, sleep, and obey the calls of nature, without ever being allowed to get out of this den."

Edwards now provisioned the mutineers' little schooner, and put on board of her a prize crew of two petty officers and seven men to navigate her as his tender. For the first few weeks, while the scent was keen, he maintained a very active search for the *Bounty*. He had three clues: first, the mention of Aitutaki in a story the mutineers had told the natives to account for their reappearance; second, a report made to him by Hillbrant, one of his prisoners, that Christian, on the night before he left Tahiti, had declared his intention of settling on Duke of York's Island; and third, the discovery on Palmerston Island of the *Bounty*'s driver yard, much worm-eaten from long immersion. It must be confessed that hopes founded on these clues did little credit to Edwards' intelligence. Aitutaki, having been discovered by Bligh, was the last place Christian would have chosen: he might have guessed that a man of Christian's intelligence would intentionally have given a false account of his projects to the mutineers he left behind, knowing that even if all who were set adrift in the boat had perished, the story of the mutiny would be learned by the first ship that visited Tahiti; a worm-eaten spar lying on the tide-mark, at an island situated directly down-wind from the Society Islands, so far from proving that the *Bounty* had been there, indicated the exact contrary. But it is to be remembered that at this time the islands known to exist in the Pacific could almost be counted on the fingers, and that Edwards could not have hoped, within the limits of a single cruise, to examine even the half of those that were marked in his chart. Had he suspected the existence of the vast number of islands around him, he would at once have realised the hopelessness of attempting to discover the hiding-place of an able navigator bent on concealment. Whether, as has been suggested by one writer,[1] Christian was piloted to Pitcairn by his Tahitian companions, of whom some were descended from the old native inhabitants, or had read of it in

1. Mr. Louis Becke, *The Mutineers*.

Carteret's voyage in 1767, or had chanced upon it by accident, he could have followed no wiser course than to steer eastward, and upwind, for any vessel despatched to arrest him would perforce go first to Tahiti for information, when it would be too late to beat to the eastward without immense loss of time.

From Aitutaki Edwards bore north-west to investigate the second clue, and in the Union Group he made his first important discovery of new land—Nukunono, inhabited by a branch of the Micronesian race, crossed with Polynesian blood. From thence he ran southward to Samoa, where he came upon traces of the massacre of La Pérouse's second in command, M. de Langle, in the shape of accoutrements cut from the uniforms of the French officers. Consistent with his usual concentration upon the object of his voyage, he does not seem to have cared to make enquiries about them.

At this stage in the voyage there occurred an accident which, from our point of view, must be regarded as the most fortunate incident of the voyage. The tender, very imperfectly victualled, parted company in a thick shower of rain. At this date Fiji, the most important group in the South Pacific, was practically unknown. Tasman had sighted its north-eastern extremity: Cook had discovered Vatoa, an outlying island in the far southward, and had heard of it from the Tongans in his second voyage when he had not time to look for it; Bligh had passed through the heart of it in his boat voyage, and had even been chased by two canoes from Round Island, Yasawa; but no European had landed or held any intercourse with the natives. It is not easy to understand how islands of such magnitude as Fiji should have remained undiscovered so long after every other important group in the Pacific had found its place in the charts of the Pacific. They were known by repute; Hamilton writes of "the savage and cannibal Feegees"; they lay but two days' sail down-wind from Tonga. Three years before the *Pandora*'s cruise the Pacific had been thrown open to the sperm whale fishery, which has had so large a part in South Sea discovery, by the cruise of the English ship *Amelia*, fitted out by Enderby; and yet neither ship of war nor whaler had chanced upon them. But for a meagre passage in Edwards' journal, and a traditional poem in the Fijian language, we should not know to whom belongs the honour of first visiting them. The native tradition sets forth that with the first visit of a European ship a devastating sickness, called the Great Lila, or wasting sickness, attacked the people of one of the Eastern Islands (of the Lau group), and, spreading from island to island, swept away vast numbers of the people. There are, it may be remarked, innumerable instances in history of the contact between continental and island peoples, both of them healthy at the time of contact, producing fatal epidemics among the islanders. Even among our own Hebrides the natives are said to look for an outbreak of *strangers' cold* after every visit of a ship. The Fijian tradition certainly dates from a few years before the beginning of the last century.

The real discoverers of Fiji seem to have been Oliver, master's mate; Renouard, midshipman; James Dodds, quartermaster, and six seamen of the *Pandora*, who formed the crew of Edwards' tender; and surely no ship that ever ventured among those dangerous islands was so ill furnished for repelling attack. Edwards had sent provisions and ammunition on board of her when off Palmerston Island, but by this time they were exhausted, and a fresh supply was actually on the *Pandora's* deck when she parted company. Her provision for the long and dangerous voyage before her was a bag of salt, a bag of nails and ironware, a boarding netting, and several seven-barrelled pieces and blunderbusses. She had besides the latitude and longitude of the places the *Pandora* would touch at.

The following account of their cruise is drawn from the remarks of Edwards and Hamilton on finding the tender safe in Samarang, for I have searched the Record Office in vain for Oliver's log. If he kept any, it was not thought worth preserving. On the night the tender parted company, the 22nd June, 1791, the natives of the south-east end of Upolu made a determined attack upon the little vessel with their canoes. The seven-barrelled pieces made terrible havoc among them, but, never having seen fire-arms, and not understanding the connection between the fall of their comrades and the report, they kept up the attack with great fury. But for the boarding netting they would easily have taken the schooner, and indeed, one fellow succeeded in springing over it, and would have felled Oliver with his club had he not been shot dead at the moment of striking. On the 23rd they cruised about in search of the *Pandora* until the afternoon when, having drunk their last drop of water, they gave her up, and made sail for Namuka, the appointed rendezvous. The torture they suffered from thirst on the passage was such that poor Renouard, the midshipman, became delirious, and continued so for many weeks. Their leeway and the easterly current combined to set them to the westward of Namuka, and the first land they made was Tofoa, which they mistook for Namuka, their rendezvous. The natives, the same that had attacked Bligh so treacherously two years before, sold them provisions and water, and then made an attempt to take the vessel, and would have succeeded but for the fire-arms. On the very day of the attack the *Pandora* dropped anchor at Namuka, within sight of Tofoa, and not finding her tender, bore down upon that island. Had Oliver been able to wait there for her, his troubles would have been at an end. But he dared not take the risk, and when Edwards sent a boat ashore to make enquiries the little schooner had sailed. The reception accorded to Edwards at Tofoa is very characteristic of the Tongans. Lieutenant Hayward, who had been present at the attack made upon Bligh, recognised several of the murderers of Norton among the people who crowded on board to do homage to the great chief, Fatafehi, who had taken passage in the frigate, but Edwards dared not punish them for fear that his tender should fall among them after he had left. Had he but known that these men had come red-handed from a treacherous attack upon the tender; that Fatafehi, who so loudly condemned their treachery to Bligh, and assured him that nothing had been seen of the little vessel, had just heard of the abortive attack they had made upon her, he would have taught them a lesson that would have lasted the Tongans many years, and might have saved the lives of the Europeans who perished in the taking of the *Port-au-Prince* and the *Duke of Portland*. For these "Norsemen of the Pacific," whom Cook, knowing nothing of the treachery they had planned against him under the guise of hospitality, misnamed the "Friendly Islanders," were, in reality, a nation of wreckers.

Leaving Tofoa about July 1st, the schooner ran westward for two days "nearly in its latitude," and fell in with an island which Edwards supposed to be one of the Fiji group. The island of the Fiji group that lies most nearly in the latitude of Tofoa is Vatoa, discovered by Cook, but there are strong reasons for seeking Oliver's discoveries elsewhere. Vatoa lies only 170 miles from Tofoa, and, therefore, if Oliver took two days in reaching it, he cannot have been running at more than three knots an hour. But, early in July, the south-east trade wind is at its strongest, and with a fair wind a fast sailer, as we know the schooner to have been, cannot have been travelling at a slower rate than six knots. We are further told that Oliver waited five weeks at the island, and took in provisions and water. Now, in July, which is the middle of the dry season, no water is to be found on Vatoa except a little muddy and fetid liquid at the bottom of shallow wells which the natives, who rely upon coconuts for drinking water, only use for cooking. Provisions also are very scarce there at all times. The same objections apply to Ongea and Fulanga which lie fifty miles north of Vatoa, in the same longitude, though they certainly possess harbours in which a vessel could lie for five weeks, which Vatoa does not. If, however, the schooner ran at the rate of six knots, as may safely be assumed, all difficulties, except that of latitude, vanish together, for at the distance of 290 nautical miles from Tofoa lies Matuku, which with much justification has been described by Wilkes as the most beautiful of all the islands in the Pacific. There the natives live in perpetual plenty among perennial streams, and could victual the largest ship without feeling any diminution of their stock. In the harbour three frigates could lie in perfect safety, and the people have earned a reputation for honesty and hospitality to passing ships which belongs to the inhabitants of none of the large islands. There is another alternative—Kandavu—but to reach that island, the schooner must have run at an average of eleven knots, and the number and cupidity of the natives would have made a stay of five weeks impossible to a vessel so poorly manned and armed.

All these considerations point to the fact that Oliver lay for five weeks at Matuku, which lies but fifty miles north of the latitude of Tofoa. He was, therefore, the first European who had intercourse with the Fijians. Their traditions have never been collected, and if one be found recording the insignificant details so dear to the native poet, such as the boarding netting, or the sickness of Midshipman Renouard, or better still, the outbreak of the Great Lila Sickness, the inference may be taken as proved.

Any other navigator than Edwards would have given us details of Oliver's wonderful voyage, or, at least, would have preserved his log, but the voyage from Fiji to the Great Barrier reef is a blank. Hamilton, indeed, alludes vaguely to the crew having had to be on their guard "at other islands that were inhabited," and since their course from Fiji to Endeavour Straits would have carried them through the heart of the New Hebrides, and close to Malicolo, we may assume that they called at Api, at Ambrym or at Malicolo to replenish their stock of water. They reached the Great Barrier reef in the greatest distress, and having run "from shore to shore," *i.e.* from New Guinea to within sight of the coast of Queensland without finding an opening, and having to choose between the alternatives of shipwreck or of death by famine, they went boldly at it, and beat over the reef. Even then they would have starved but for their providential encounter with a small Dutch vessel cruising a little to the westward of Endeavour Straits, which supplied them with water and provisions. The governor of the first Dutch settlement they touched at, having a description of the mutineers from the British Government, and observing that their schooner was built of foreign timber, refused to believe their account of themselves, especially as Oliver, being a petty officer, could produce no commission or warrant in support of his statement, and imprisoned them all, without, however, treating them with harshness. On the first opportunity he sent them to Samarang, where Edwards had them released. The plucky little schooner was sold, to begin another career of usefulness and her purchase money was divided among the *Pandora*'s crew.

Thus ended one of the most eventful voyages in the history of South Sea discovery, dismissed by Edwards in a few lines; by Hamilton in two pages. The search made among the naval archives at the Record Office leaves but little hope that any log-book or journal has been preserved.

Meanwhile, Edwards, disappointed in his search for the tender at Namuka and Tofoa, and prevented by a head wind from examining Tongatabu, set his course again for Samoa, and passed within sight of Vavau by the way. Making the easterly extremity of the group, he visited in turn Manua, Tutuila, and Upolu, but, like Bougainville, did not sight Savaii, which lay a little to the northward of his course. It is not surprising that the natives of Upolu denied all knowledge of the tender, seeing that they had made a determined attempt upon her less than a month before. From Samoa he sailed to Vavau which he named Howe's Group, in ignorance that it had been discovered by Maurelle ten years before, and subsequently visited by La Pérouse. Running south-ward, he made Pylstaart, at that time inhabited by Tongan casta-ways, and the fact that he did not stop to examine it, although he saw by the smoke that it was inhabited, shows that he had begun to tire of his search for the mutineers. Having enquired at Tongatabu and Eua, he returned to Namuka for water, and at this point any systematic search either for the tender or the mutineers seems to have been abandoned.

Edwards had now been nine months at sea, and the prospect of the long homeward voyage round the Cape was still before him. With every league he had sailed westward the scent had grown fainter, and he was about to pass the spot from which the muti-neers were known to have sailed in the opposite direction. His course is not easy to explain. To reason that the tender had fallen to leeward of her rendezvous, and had been compelled to seek shelter and provisions at one of the islands discovered by Bligh only two days' sail to the westward, required no high degree of foresight; and yet Edwards, who must have known the position of the Fiji islands from Bligh's narrative, deliberately set his course for Niuatobutabu, two days' sail to the north-west. But, falling to leeward of it, he made Niuafo'ou, the curious volcanic island discovered by Schouten in 1616, and never since visited. The prevailing wind making a visit to Niuatobutabu now impossible, he visited Wallis Island, and then bore away to the west.

On August 8th, 1791, he made the discovery of Rotuma, whose enterprising people now furnish the Torres Straits pearl fishery with its best divers. It is difficult to forgive him for leaving so meagre an account of this interesting little community of mixed Polynesian and Micronesian blood. Edwards was probably mistaken in thinking their intentions hostile. Kau Moala, a Tongan who visited them in 1807, and related his experiences to Mariner, describes them as always friendly to strangers. Probably they took the *Pandora* for a god-ship, and since the Immortals of their Pantheon are generally malevolent, they left their women behind, and flourished weapons to scare the gods into good behaviour. In 1807 they had forgotten the visit, perhaps because it had brought them no calamity to inspire the native poets. Hamilton relates an incident quite in keeping with the character of this determined and sturdy little people.

> One fellow was making off with some booty, but was detected; and although five of the stoutest men in the ship were hanging upon him, and had fast hold of his long flowing black hair, he overpowered them all, and jumped overboard with his prize.

The ill fortune that pursued Edwards, that had baulked him of Pitcairn when it lay within a few hours' sail, that had cheated him at once of the recovery of his tender and the discovery of Fiji, and was soon to rob him of his ship, now dealt him the unkindest cut of all. On August 13th, he sighted the island of Vanikoro, and ran along its shore, sometimes within a mile of the reef. There was no conceivable reason why he should not have made some attempt to communicate with the inhabitants whose smoke signals attracted his attention. Had he done so, he would have been the means of rescuing the survivors of La Pérouse's expedition, and of clearing away the mystery that covered their fate for so many years. For, after Dillon's discoveries, there can be little doubt that they were on the island at that very time, and it is not unlikely that the smoke was actually a signal made by them to attract his attention. The Comte de la Pérouse, who had been despatched on a voyage of discovery by Louis XVI. on the eve of the Revolution, handed his journals to Governor Phillip in Botany Bay for transmission to Europe in 1788, and neither he, nor his two frigates, nor any of their company were ever seen again. Their fate produced so painful an impression in France that the National Assembly, then in the throes of the Revolution, sent out a relief expedition under Citizen-Admiral d'Entrecasteaux, and issued a splendid edition of his journals at the public expense. We now know from the native account elicited by Dillon that during a hurricane on a very dark night both frigates struck on the reef of Vanikoro, that the *Astrolabe* foundered with all hands in deep water, and the crew of the *Boussole* got safe to land. They stayed on the island until they had built a brig of native timber, in which they sailed away to the westward to meet a second shipwreck, perhaps on the Great Barrier reef. But two of them stayed behind for many years, and of these one was certainly alive in 1825. Now, Edwards saw Vanikoro just three years after the wreck, and even if the brig had sailed, there were two castaways who could have cleared up the mystery.

After a narrow escape from shipwreck on the Indispensable Reef, he made the coast of New Guinea, supposing it to be one of the Louisiades. And here has occurred one of those curious errors in geographical nomenclature which are perpetuated by the most permanent of all histories—the Admiralty charts. Edwards gives the positions of two conspicuous headlands, which he named Cape Rodney and Cape Hood, and of a mountain lying between them which he called Mount Clarence. All these names appear in the Admiralty charts, but they are assigned to the wrong places. To a ship coming from the eastward the Cape Rodney of the charts is not conspicuous enough to have attracted Edwards' attention. The Cape Hood of the charts, on the contrary, cannot be mistaken, and it lies exactly in the position which Edwards gave for Cape Rodney. The Cape Hood that Edwards saw was undoubtedly Round Head, and his Mount Clarence must have been the high cone between them in the

Saroa district. The *Pandora* must have approached on one of those misty mornings when the clouds creep down the mountain sides of New Guinea, and obscure the ranges that rise, tier upon tier, right up to the towering peak of Mount Victoria, or Edwards could not have mistaken the continent for the insignificant islands of the Louisiades. On such a morning a narrow line of coast stands out clear against a background of sombre fog.

The baleful fortune of the *Pandora*, now folded her wings and perched upon the taffrail. By hugging the coast of New Guinea she would have won a clear passage through these wreck-strewn straits of Torres, but the navigators of those days counted on clear water to Endeavour Straits, and recked little of the dangers of the Great Barrier reef. Bligh, who chanced upon a passage in 12.34 S. Lat. so aptly that he called it Providential Channel, cautioned future navigators in words that should have warned Edwards against the course he was steering. "These, however, are marks too small for a ship to hit, unless it can hereafter be ascertained that passages through the reef are numerous along the coast." Edwards was not looking for Bligh's passage, which lay more than two degrees southward of his course. He had lately adopted a most dangerous practice of running blindly on through the night. Until he made the coast of New Guinea, he had profited by the warning of Bougainville, the only navigator whose book he seems to have studied, and always lay to till daylight, but now, in the most dangerous sea in the world, he threw this obvious precaution to the wind. Hamilton, to whom we are indebted for this information (for it did not transpire at the court martial) says that "the great length of the voyage would not permit it." How fatuous a proceeding it was in unsurveyed and unknown waters may be judged from the fact that in coral seas that have been carefully surveyed all ships of war are now compelled to keep the lead going whenever they move in coral waters. On August 25th he discovered the Murray Islands, and, after spending the day in a vain attempt to force a passage through them, he followed the reef southward for two days without finding a passage. This must have brought him very near the latitude of Bligh's passage. On the morning of August 28th Lieutenant Corner was sent to examine what appeared to be a channel, and an hour before dark he signalled that he had found a passage large enough for the ship. The night fell before the boat could get back, and this induced Edwards, who had already lost one boat's crew and his tender, to lie much closer to the reef than was prudent. The current did the rest. About seven the ship struck heavily, and, bumping over the reef, tore her planking so that, despite eleven hours incessant pumping, she foundered shortly after daylight. Eighty-nine of the ship's company and ten of the mutineers were picked up by the boats and landed on a sand cay four miles distant, and thirty-one sailors, and four mutineers (who went down in manacles) were drowned.

Having read the different versions of this affair both for and against Edwards, I think it is proved that, besides treating his prisoners with inhumanity, he disregarded the orders of the Admiralty. His attitude towards the prisoners was always consistent. We learn from Corner that he allowed Coleman, Norman and Mackintosh to work at the pumps, but that when the others implored him to let them out of irons he placed two additional sentries over them, and threatened to shoot the first man who attempted to liberate himself. Every allowance must be made for the fear that in the disordered state of the ship, they might have made an attempt to escape, but during the eleven hours in which the water was gaining upon the pumps there was ample time to provide for their security. That so many were saved was due, not to him, but to a boatswain's mate, who risked his own life to liberate them. Lieutenant Corner, who would not have been likely to err on the side of hostility to Edwards, gives his evidence against him in this particular. But whether he is to be believed or not, the fact that four of the prisoners went down in irons is impossible to extenuate.

Edwards dismisses the boat voyage in very few words, though, in fact, it was a remarkable achievement to take four overloaded boats from the Barrier Reef to Timor without the loss of a single man. He made the coast of Queensland a little to the south of Albany Island, where the blacks first helped him to fill his water breakers, and then attacked him. He watered again at Horn Island, and then sailed through the passage which bears Flinders' name owing to the fallacy that he discovered it. After clearing the sound, he seems to have mistaken Prince of Wales' Island for Cape York, which he had left many miles behind him.

Favoured by a fair wind and a calm sea, he made the run from Flinders passage to Timor in eleven days. Like Bligh, he found that the young bore their privations better than the old, and that the first effect of thirst and famine is to make men excessively irritable. Hamilton records a characteristic incident. Edwards had neglected to conduct prayers in his boat until he was reminded of his duty by one of the mutineers, who was leading the devotions of the seamen in the bows of the boat. Scandalized at the impropriety of a pirate daring to appeal to the Highest Tribunal for mercy, as it were, behind the back of the earthly court before which he was shortly to be arraigned, the captain sternly reproved him, and conducted prayers himself. A sense of humour was not numbered among Edwards' endowments.

Timor was sighted on the 13th September, and on the 15th the party landed at Coupang, where the Dutch authorities received them with every hospitality. Here they met the survivors of a third boat voyage, scarcely less adventurous than Bligh's and their own. A party of convicts, including a woman and two small children, had contrived to steal a ship's gig and to escape in her from Port Jackson. Sleeping on shore at nights whenever possible, subsisting on shell-fish and sea-birds, they ran the entire length of the Queensland coast, threaded Endeavour Straits, and arrived at Coupang after an exposure lasting ten weeks without the loss of a single life. Having given themselves out as the survivors from the wreck of an English ship, they were entertained with great hospitality until the arrival of Edwards two weeks later, when they betrayed their story gratuitously. The captain of a Dutch vessel, who spoke English, on first hearing the news of Edwards' landing, ran to them with the glad tidings of their captain's arrival, on which one of them started up in surprise and exclaimed, "What captain? Dam'me! we have no captain."

On hearing this the governor had them arrested, and sent to the castle, one man and the woman having to be pursued into the bush before they were taken. They then confessed that they were escaped convicts.

Apart from their adventurous voyage, there is much romance about their story. William Bryant, the leader, had been transported for smuggling, and his sweetheart, Mary Broad, who was maid to a lady in Salcombe, in Devonshire for connivance in her lover's escape from Winchester Gaol. In due course they were married in Botany Bay, where Bryant was employed as fisherman to the governor, a post that enabled him to plan their successful escape. Bryant and both children died on the voyage home, together with three others, Morton, Cox and Simms, but the woman survived to obtain a full pardon, owing chiefly to the exertions of an officer of marines who went home with her in the *Gorgon*, and eventually married her.[2] Butcher, who was also pardoned, returned to New South Wales and became a thriving settler. The remaining four were sent back to complete their sentences. Their story has been graphically told by Messrs. Louis Becke and Walter Jeffery in *The First Fleet Family*.

During the voyage from Coupang to Batavia Edwards narrowly escaped a second shipwreck. The *Rembang* was dismasted on a lee shore in a cyclone, and, but for the exertions of the English seamen, would assuredly have been stranded, the Dutch sailors, who, says the facetious Hamilton, "would fight the devil should he appear to them in any other shape but that of thunder and lightning," having taken to their hammocks. At Samarang, as already related, Edwards found the tender, which he had long given up for lost, and the price she fetched enabled the crew to purchase decent clothing. Heywood afterwards asserted that no clothing was given to the prisoners but what they could earn by plaiting and selling straw hats. They were miserably housed, when on board the *Rembang*, and kept

---

2. The *Gorgon* also carried Lieutenant Clark, of the Royal Marines, whose journal of the voyage to Botany Bay and Norfolk Island in 1789 throws a very interesting light upon the early days of the colony. Unfortunately the journal says very little of the *Gorgon*'s voyage home.

in rigid confinement both at Batavia, and on the *Vreedemberg*, in which they made the voyage to the Cape.

At Batavia Edwards divided his men among three Dutch vessels homeward bound, but at the Cape he removed his own contingent into H.M.S. *Gorgon*, and arrived at Spithead on June 18th, 1792. Two days later the ten mutineers were transferred to H.M.S. *Hector*, Captain Montague, and the convicts were sent to Newgate. The court martial, which did not assemble until September 12th, lasted five days, with the result that Norman, Coleman, Mackintosh and Byrne were acquitted, and Heywood, Morrison, Ellison, Burkitt, Millward and Muspratt were condemned to death, the two first being recommended to mercy. On October 24th Heywood and Morrison received the King's pardon, and both re-entered the navy, Heywood to retire in 1816, when nearly at the head of the list of captains; Morrison to go down in the ill-fated *Blenheim* in which he was serving as gunner. Muspratt also was pardoned, but the three others were hanged on board the *Brunswick* in Portsmouth Harbour on October 29th, 1792. Thus ended a voyage that, for adventure and discovery, deserves a high place in the history of maritime enterprise in the Pacific. Voyages take their rank from the scientific attainments and literary ability of the men who record them, and the *Pandora*, unlucky in her fate as in her ill-omened name, was scarcely less unfortunate in her historian.

B. T.

Captain Edwards' Reports

Captain Edwards' Reports

Sir, Be pleased to acquaint My Lords Commissioners of the Admiralty that I sailed again from Jack-in-the-Basket with His Majesty's Ship *Pandora* under my command on the 7th day of November, and anchored in Santa Cruz by Tenerife on the 22nd: that nothing particular occurred in my passage to this place, except that of my falling in with His Majesty's sloop *Shark* on the 17th November in Latitude 32° 33' Longitude 13° 40'W. bound to Madeira with despatches for Rear Admiral Cornish, and my learning from them that the matters in dispute with Spain were amicably settled, of which circumstance I was unacquainted when I left England. I am now completing my water, and have taken on board full 3 months wine for my compliment, with some fruit and vegetables, and purpose and flatter myself that I shall be able to sail from hence this evening. Enclosed I send the state and condition of His Majesty's Ship *Pandora* for their Lordships' information, and I have the honour to be, Sir,

Your most obedient and ever humble servant,
Edward Edwards
Phillip Stevens, Esq.

PANDORA, AT RIO DE JANEIRO
6TH JANUARY, 1791

Sir, Be pleased to acquaint My Lords Commissioners of the Admiralty that I sailed from Tenerife with His Majesty's Ship *Pandora* on the afternoon of the 25th November, agreeable to my intentions signified to their Lordships by letter from that island, and anchored off the city Rio Janeiro on the evening of the 31st of December with a view to complete my water and to get refreshments for the ship's company and from my being persuaded that very long runs, particularly with new ships' companies, are prejudicial to health, and as my men are of that description, and have also suffered in their health from a fever which has prevailed amongst them in a greater or less degree ever since they left England, were other inducements for my touching at this port. I shall stay here no longer than is absolutely necessary to procure these articles, and which I expect to be able to accomplish by the seventh of this month, and I shall then proceed on my voyage as soon as wind and weather will permit.

Herewith I send the state and condition of His Majesty's Ship *Pandora,* and I have the honour to be, Sir,

Your most obedient and humble servant,
Edward Edwards

BATAVIA
25TH NOVEMBER, 1791
(29TH MAY, 1792 FROM AMSTERDAM)

Sir, In a letter dated the 6th day of January, 1791, which I did myself the honour to address to you from Rio Janeiro I gave an account of my proceedings up to that time and enclosed the state and condition of His Majesty's Ship *Pandora* under my command, and having completed the water and procured such articles of provision, etc., for the use of the ship's company as they were in want of and I thought necessary for the voyage, I sailed from that port on the 8th January, 1791, run along the coast of America, Tierra Del Fuego, Hatin Land, round Cape Horn and proceeded directly to Otaheite, and arrived at Matavy Bay in that Island on the 23rd March without having touched in any other place in my passage thither.

It was my intention to have put into New Year's harbour, or some other port in its neighbourhood to complete our water and to refresh my people, could I have effected that business within the month of January; but as I arrived too late on that coast to fulfil my intentions within the time, it determined me to push forward without delay, by which means I flattered myself I might avoid that extreme bad weather and all the evil consequences that are usually experienced in doubling Cape Horn in a more advanced season of the year, and I had the good fortune not to be disappointed in my expectation.

After doubling the Cape, and advancing Northward into warmer weather, the fever which had prevailed on board gradually declined, and the diseases usually succeeding such fevers prevented by a liberal use of the *antiscorbutics* and other nourishing and useful articles with which we were so amply supplied, and the ship's company arrived at Otaheite in perfect health, except a few whose debilitated constitutions no climate, provisions or medicine could much improve.

In our run to Otaheite we discovered 3 islands: the first, which I called Ducie's Island, lies in Latitude 24° 40' 30" S. and Longitude 124° 36' 30" W. from Greenwich. It is between 2 and 3 miles long. The second I called Lord Hood's Island. It lies in Latitude 21° 31' S. and Longitude 135° 32' 30" W., and is about 8 miles long. The third I called Carysfort's Island. It lies in Latitude 20° 49' S. and Longitude 138° 33' W. and it is 5 miles long. They are all three low lagoon islands covered with wood, but we saw no inhabitants on either of them.[1] Before we anchored at Matavy Bay, Joseph Coleman, armourer of the *Bounty*, and several of the natives came on board, from whom I learned that Christian the pirate had landed and left 16 of his men on the Island, some of whom were then at Matavy, and some had sailed from there the morning before our arrival (in a schooner they had built) for Papara, a distant part of the Island, to join other of the pirates that were settled at that place, and that Churchill, master at arms, had been murdered by Matthew Thompson, and that Matthew Thompson was killed by the natives and offered as a sacrifice on their altars for the murder of Churchill, whom they had made a chief.

George Stewart and Peter Heywood, midshipmen of the *Bounty*, came on board the *Pandora* soon after she came to an anchor, and I had also information that Richard Skinner was at Matavy. I desired Poen, an inferior chief (who, in the absence of Otoo, was the principal person in the district) to bring him on board. The chief went on shore for the purpose, and soon after he returned again and informed me that Skinner was coming on board. Before night he did come on board, but whether it was in consequence of the chief's instructions, or his own accord, I am at a loss to say. As soon as the ship was moored the pinnace and launch were got ready and sent under the direction of Lieutenant Corner and Hayward in pursuit of the pirates and schooner in hopes of getting hold of them before they could get information of our arrival, and Odiddee, a native of Bolabola, and who has been with Captain Cook, etc., went with them as a guide.

The boats were discovered by the pirates before they had arrived at the place where these people had landed, and they immediately embarked in their schooner and put to sea, and she was chased the remainder of the day by our boats, but, it blowing fresh, she outsailed them, and the boats returned to the ship. Jonathan Brown, the person left at Otaheite by Mr. Cox of the *Mercury*,[2] and from whom their Lordships supposed I might get some useful information, had been under the necessity for his own safety to associate with the pirates, but he took the opportunity to leave them when they were about to embark in the schooner and put to sea. He informed me that

1. They sighted Easter Island on March 4th, 1791, Ducie's Island on the 16th, Hoods' Island on the 17th, and Carysfort on the 19th. The latitude and description of Ducie's Island leaves little doubt that it was the first island discovered by Quiros on January 26th, 1606 and called by him Luna Puesta. It appears as Encarnaçion in Espinosa's chart. Quiros thus describes it: *"A buen juzgar dista de Lima ochocientas leguas: tiene cinco de boj, mucha arboleda y playas de arena, y junto á tierra fondo de ochenta brazas."* Had Edwards but sailed due west from Ducie Island he must have sighted Pitcairn and discovered the hiding-place of Fletcher Christian's ill-fated colony.
2. An American vessel.

they had very little water and provisions on board, or vessels to hold them in, and, of course, could not keep at sea long. I entered Brown on the ship's books as part of the compliment and found him very intelligent and useful in the different capacities of guide, soldier and seaman. I employed different people to look out for and to give information on their landing either on this or the neighbouring islands.

On the 26th, in the evening, sent the pinnace to Edee by desire of the old Otoo, or king, to bring him on board the *Pandora*. Early on the morning of the 27th, I had information that the pirates were returning with the schooner to Papara and that they were landed and retired to the mountains, to endeavour to conceal and defend themselves. Immediately sent Lt. Corner with 26 men in the launch to Papara to pursue them. At night the Otoo, his two queens and suite came on board the pinnace and slept on board the *Pandora*, which they afterwards frequently did.

The next morning Lieutenant Hayward was sent with a party in the pinnace to join the party in the launch at Papara. I found the Otoo ready to furnish me with guides and to give me any other assistance in his power, but he had very little authority or influence in that part of the island where the pirates had taken refuge, and even his right to the sovereignty of the eastern part of the island had been recently disputed by Tamarie, one of the royal family. Under these circumstances I conceived the taking of the Otoo and the other chiefs attached to his interest into custody would alarm the faithful part of his subjects and operate to our disadvantage. I therefore satisfied myself with the assistance he offered and had in his power to give me, and I found means at different times to send presents to Tamarie (and invited him to come on board, which he promised to do, but never fulfilled his promise), and convinced him I had it in my power to lay his country in waste, which I imagined would be sufficient at least to make him withhold that support he hitherto, through policy, had occasionally given to the pirates in order to draw them to his interest and to strengthen his own party against the Otoo.

I probably might have had it in my power to have taken and secured the person of Tamarie, but I was apprehensive that such an attempt might irritate the natives attached to his interest, and induce them to act hostilely against our party at a time the ship was at too great a distance to afford them timely and necessary assistance in case of such an event, and I adopted the milder method for that reason, and from a persuasion that our business could be brought to a conclusion at less risk and in less time by that means. The yawl was sent to Papara with spare hands to bring back the launch which was wanted to water the ship, and on the 29th the launch returned to the ship with James Morrison,[3] Charles Norman, and Thomas Ellison, belonging to the *Bounty*, and who had been made prisoners at Papara on the 7th April. The companies returned with the detachment from Papara, and brought with them the pirate schooner which they had taken there. The natives had deserted the place, and I had information that the six remaining pirates had fled to the mountains.

On the 5th I sent Lieutenant Hayward with 25 men in the schooner and yawl to Papara, the old Otoo and several of the youths, &c., went with him. On the 7th, in the morning, Lieutenant Corner was landed with 16 men at Point Venus in order to march round the back of the mountains, in which the pirates had retreated, to cooperate with the party sent to Papara. Oris-

3. Morrison was Boatswain's Mate of the *Bounty*. He had previously served as midshipman in the navy, and by talent and education he was far above the station he held in Bligh's ship. It was he who planned and directed the building of the fast-sailing little schooner which acted as the *Pandora's* tender, was the first vessel to anchor in Fiji, and made the record passage from China to the Sandwich Islands. Morrison was chaplain as well as foreman to the little band of shipwrights. On Sundays he hoisted the English colours on a staff and read the Church Service to them. He kept a journal, not only throughout the *Bounty's* cruise, but during his sojourn with the mutineers in Tahiti, and, though it is not explained how he contrived to preserve it through the wreck of the *Pandora* and the boat voyage, there can be no doubt that it was a genuine document. At Captain Heywood's death it passed with his other papers to his daughters. This journal has been annotated and corrected by another hand, probably Heywood's own, but without material alteration of the sense. It is filled with acrimony against Bligh from the outset of the *Bounty's* cruise, and the form of the entries shows that it was intended to be the basis for laying serious charges against him when the ship was paid off. It is needless to add that it does not spare Edwards in respect of his treatment of his prisoners.

sia, the Otoo's brother, and a party of natives went with him as guides and to carry the provisions, &c.

On the 9th Lieutenant Hayward returned with the schooner and yawl and brought with him Henry Hillbrant, Thomas M'Intosh, Thomas Burkitt, Jonathan Millward, Jonathan Sumner and William Muspratt, the six remaining pirates belonging to the *Bounty*. They had quitted the mountains and had got down near the seashore when they were discovered by our party on the opposite side of a river. They submitted, on being summoned to lay down their arms. Lieutenant Corner with his party marched across the mountains to Papara, and a boat was sent for them there, and they returned on board again on the 13th in the afternoon. I put the pirates in the round house which I built at the after part of the Quarter deck for their more effectual security, airy and healthy situation, and to separate them from, and to prevent their having any communication with, or to crowd and incommode the ship's company.

Contrary to my expectations, the water we got at the usual place at Point Venus turned out very bad, and on touching for better, most excellent water was found issuing out of a rock in a little bay to the southward of One Tree Hill. I mention this circumstance because it may be of importance to be known to other ships that may hereafter touch at that island.

The natives had in their possession a bower anchor belonging to the *Bounty*, which that ship had left in the bay, and I took it on board the *Pandora*, and made them a handsome present by way of salvage and as a reward for their ingenuity in weighing it with materials so ill calculated for the purpose. I learned from different people and from journals kept on board the *Bounty*, which were found in the chests of the pirates at Otaheite, that after Lieutenant Bligh and the people with him were turned adrift in the launch, the pirates proceeded with the ship to the Island of Toobouai in Latitude 20° 13' S. and Longitude 149° 35' W., where they anchored on the 25th May, 1789. Before their arrival there they threw the greatest part of the bread fruit plants overboard, and the property of the officers and people that were turned out of the ship was divided amongst those who remained on board her, and the royals and some other small sails were cut up and disposed of in the same manner.

Notwithstanding they met with some opposition from the natives, they intended to settle on this island, but after some time they perceived that they were in want of several things necessary for a settlement and which was the cause of disagreements and quarrels amongst themselves. At last they came to a resolution to come to Otaheite to get such of the things wanted as could be procured there, and in consequence of that resolution they sailed from Toobouai at the latter end of the month and arrived at Otaheite on the 6th of June. The Otoo and other natives were very inquisitive and desirous to know what was become of Lieutenant Bligh and the other absentees and the bread fruit plants, &c. They deceived them by saying that they had fallen in with Captain Cook at an island he had lately discovered called Why-Too-Tackee, and where he intended to settle, and that the plants were landed and planted there, and that Lieutenant Bligh and the other absentees were detained to assist Captain Cook in the business he had in hand, and that he had appointed Christian captain of the *Bounty* and ordered him to Otaheite for an additional supply of hogs, goats, fowls, bread fruit plants, &c.

These humane islanders were imposed upon by this artful story, and they were so rejoiced to hear that their old friend Captain Cook was alive and was near them that they used every means in their power to procure the things that were wanted, so that in the course of a few days the *Bounty* took on board 312 hogs, 38 goats, eight dozen fowls, a bull and a cow, and a quantity of bread fruit plants, &c. They also took with them a woman, eight men and seven boys. With these supplies they sailed from Otaheite on the 19th June and arrived again at Toobouai on the 26th. They landed the live stock on the quays that were near the harbour, lightened the ship and warped her up the harbour into two fathoms water opposite to the place where they intended to build the fort. On this occasion their spare masts, yards and booms were got out and moored, but they afterwards broke adrift and were lost.[4]

---

4. The *Pandora* found one of them at Palmerston Island.

On the 19th July they began to build the fort. Its dimensions were 50 yards square. These villains had frequent quarrels amongst themselves which at last were carried to such a length that no order was observed amongst them, and by the 30th August the work at the fort was discontinued. They had also almost continual disputes and skirmishes with the natives, which were generally brought on by their own violence and depredations. Christian, perceiving that he had lost his authority, and that nothing more could be done, desired them to consult together and consider what step would be the most advisable to take, and said that he would put into execution the opinion that was supported by the most votes. After long consultation it was at last determined that the scheme of staying at Toobouai should be given up, and that the ship should be taken to Otaheite, where those who chose to go on shore should be at liberty to do so, and those who remained on the ship might take her away to whatever place they should think fit.

In consequence of this final determination preparations were made for the purpose and they sailed from Toobouai on the 15th and arrived at Matavy Bay, Otaheite, on the 20th September 1789. The bull which they took from Otaheite died on its passage to Toobouai, and they killed the cow before they left that island, yet, notwithstanding this and the depredations they committed there, the natives still derived considerable advantage from their visits, as several hogs, goats, fowls and other things of their introduction were left behind. These sixteen men mentioned before were landed at Otaheite, *viz.*:

Name	Position	Ultimately
Joseph Coleman	Armourer	Acquitted
George Stewart	Midshipman	Drowned in *Pandora* wreck
Michael Burn	A.B. Fiddler	Acquitted
Charles Norman	Carpenter's Mate	Acquitted
Henry Hillbrant	A.B.	Drowned in *Pandora* wreck
Thomas M'Intosh	Carpenter's Crew	Acquitted
Thomas Burkitt	A.B.	Executed at Portsmouth
Peter Heywood	Midshipman	Pardoned

Richard Skinner	A.B.	Drowned in *Pandora* wreck
James Morrison	Boatswain's Mate	Pardoned
Thomas Ellison	A.B.	Executed at Portsmouth
John Sumner	A.B.	Drowned in *Pandora* wreck
William Muspratt	A.B.	Executed at Portsmouth
John Millward	A.B.	Executed at Portsmouth

These fourteen were made prisoners by my people and Charles Churchill and Matthew Thompson were murdered on that island. Previous to these people being put on shore the small arms, powder, canvas and the small stores belonging to the ship were equally divided amongst the whole crew. After building the schooner six of these people actually sailed in her for the East Indies, but meeting with bad weather and suspecting the abilities of Morrison, whom they had chosen to be their captain to navigate her there, they returned again to Otaheite on the night between the 21st and 22nd of September 1789 and were seen in the morning to the N.W. of Point Venus.[5]

Fletcher Christian, Edward Young, Matthew Quintall, William M'Koy, Alexander Smith, John Williams, Isaac Martin, William Brown and John Mills went away in the ship and they also took with them several natives of these islands, both men and women, but I could not exactly learn their numbers, only that they had on board a few more women than white men, a deficiency of whom had formerly been one of their grievances and the principal cause of their quarrels. Christian had been frequently heard to declare that he would search for an unknown or uninhabited island in which there was no harbour for shipping, would run the ship ashore and get from her such things as would be useful to him and settle there, but this information

---

5. Morrison said that his plan was to reach Batavia in time to secure a passage home in the next fleet bound to Holland, and that the return to Tahiti was occasioned, not by any distrust of his talents, but by the refusal of the natives, who were anxious to keep them in Tahiti, to victual the ship for so long a voyage. There were no casks on the schooner for storing water. Morrison, Heywood and Stewart had planned an escape from Tubuai in the *Bounty*'s boat, but, fortunately for them—since the attempt would have been certain death—their plan was discovered and frustrated by the other mutineers.

was too vague to be followed in an immense ocean strewed with an almost innumerable number of known and unknown islands; therefore after the ship was caulked, which I found was necessary to be done, the rigging overhauled and in other respects refitted her for sea, and fitted the pirates' schooner as a tender, and put on board two petty officers[6] and seven men to navigate her, conceiving she would be of considerable use in covering the boats in my future search for the *Bounty*, as well as for reconnoitring the passage through the reef leading to Endeavour Straits; I sailed from Otaheite on the 8th of May with a view to put the remainder of my orders into execution.

Oediddee was desirous to go in the *Pandora* to Ulietia and to Bolabola, and as I thought he would be useful as a guide for the boats I took him with me and steered for Huahaine which we saw the next morning. The tender and the boats were employed the 9th and part of the 10th in examining the harbours, and Oediddee went with them as pilot. Several chiefs came on board and brought with them hogs and other articles, the produce of the island, and a servant of Omai also came on board, and said that he was not then much the better for his master's riches, however his former connections was the cause of his visit to the ship being made very profitable to him, and all the chiefs and their attendances received presents from me. Two of the chiefs of this island were desirous to go in the ship to Ulietia and I had given them leave to, but when the ship was about to make sail they suddenly changed their minds and went on shore and took Oediddee with them. Oediddee promised to follow us there the next day, but we did not see him again.

I proceeded to Ulietea Otaka and Bolabola, and the tender and boats were employed in examining the bays and harbours of these islands, but we got no intelligence of the *Bounty* or her people. Tahatoo, who called himself king of Bolabola, informed me that he had been a few days before at Tubai, which is a small, low island situated on the Northward of Bolabola and under its jurisdiction, and that there were no white men upon that island, nor

---

6. Oliver, master's mate; Renouard, midshipman; James Dodds, quartermaster; and six seamen.

upon Maurua, another island in sight of it and to the westward of Bolabola. He also mentioned another island which I thought he called Mojeshah, but we know no such island unless it be Howe's Island, and that seems to be situated too far to the South and to the West for the island he attempted to describe and point out to us. The chiefs and several other people came on board from these islands and brought with them the usual produce, and they were at all the isles very pressing to prevail upon us to make a longer stay with them, but as I had no object particularly in view and my people in good health, I did not think it proper unnecessarily to waste my time for the sake of procuring a few articles that were in greater abundance in these islands than at Otaheite. I made presents to all those chiefs as it was my custom to do to everyone that had the least pretension to pre-eminence, and to all the people who came on board in the first boat.

After leaving Bolabola I steered for Maurua and passed it at a small distance. Howe's Island was not seen by us as it is a low island and we passed to the Southward of it. I then shaped my course to get into the latitude of and to fall in to the Eastward of Why-to-tackee.

On the 14th, Henry Hillbrant, one of the pirates, gave information that Christian had declared to him the evening before he left Otaheite that he intended to go with the *Bounty* to an uninhabited island discovered by Mr. Byron, situated to the Westward of the Isles of Danger, which, from description of the situation, I found to be the island called by Mr. Byron the Duke of York's Island,[7] and if they could land, would settle there and run the ship upon the reef and destroy her, and if they could not land, or if on examination found it would not answer their purpose, he would look out for some other uninhabited island. However, I continued my course for Why-to-tackee, being now determined to examine the island in preference to following

7. Oatafu, one of the Union Group, discovered by Commodore Byron in 1765. If the mutineers had settled there they would have starved, for there is neither food nor water. Since Byron's discovery a native settlement has been made from Bowditch Island (Fakaago), and the people, about 100 in number, live on fish, *pandanus*, and water caught in holes cut on the lee side of the cocoa-palms.

any intelligence, however plausible, and on the morning of the 19th saw the Island of Why-to-tackee,[8] and sent the tender in shore to ground and look out for a harbour.

At noon sent Lieutenant Hayward in the yawl to look into a place on the N.W. part of the island that had the appearance of a harbour and to get intelligence of the natives. In the evening he returned. The place was so far from being fit for the reception of the ship that he could scarcely find a passage through the reef for the boat; he conversed with seven or eight different sets of people, whom he met with in canoes, and they all agreed that

---

8. The northernmost island of the Cook Group, discovered by Bligh, April 11, 1798, a few days before the mutiny. In 1823 John Williams, the missionary, heard at Rarotonga a native tradition of Bligh's visit. The natives heard the first rumours of a world beyond their own from two Tahitian castaways who had seen Captain Cook, and had with them an iron hatchet obtained from the *Resolution*. They represented the strange beings who traversed the ocean in vast canoes, not lashed with *sinnet* nor furnished with outriggers, as impious people who laughed at the taboo, and even ate of the consecrated food from the Maraés. They were like the gods; if they were attacked they blew at their assailants with long blow-pipes (*pupuhi*) from which flames and stones were belched. Such were the Tutë (Cooks). Thereafter, having need of iron (*kurima*) and other wonders current in Tahiti the men of Aitutaki prayed to their gods to send the Tutë to their island with axes and nails and *pupuhi*, and this, according to an old priest, was their prayer. "O great Tangaroa, send your large ship to our land: let us see the Cookees. Great Tangiia, send us a dead sea, send us a propitious gale, to bring the far-famed Cookees to our land, to give us nails and iron and axes; let us see these outriggerless canoes." And with the feast presented with the prayer were promises of greater feasts so soon as their prayer was answered. The gods heard them. A few months later the Cookees came. The great ship did not anchor, but one of the natives took his courage in both hands, and went off in his canoe. He brought back strange tales of what he had seen. It was a floating island; there were two rivers flowing on it (the pumps), and two plantations in which grew taro and sugar-cane and bread-fruit, and the keel scraped the bottom of the sea, for he dived as deep as he could go without finding it. Williams has fallen into two errors in his account In the same breath he claims for himself the discovery of Rarotonga, in 1823, and announces this to have been a visit of the *Bounty* after she was taken by the mutineers, *i.e.* in April, 1789. Rarotonga was, in fact, discovered by the ship *Seringapatam* in 1814, though Williams may have been the first to land. The tradition must have referred to Bligh's visit to Aitutaki before the mutiny when the decks were encumbered with bread-fruit, for we know that the first thing the mutineers did after setting their captain adrift was to throw all the bread-fruit plants overboard, and that they steered direct for Tahiti.

the *Bounty* was not, nor had not been there since Lieutenant Bligh left the island, nor did any of them known anything of her. Lieutenant Hayward recollected one of the natives, whom he remembered to have seen on board the *Bounty* when he discovered the island, and he saw another savage belonging to a neighbouring island who knew Captain Cook and inquired after him, Omai and Oediddee, whom he said he had seen.

These people at first approached the boat with caution, and could not be prevailed upon to come on board the ship. As I was convinced that the *Bounty* was not on this island, and as Hervey's, Mangea and Wattea Islands to the S.E. of Why-to-tac-kee were inhabited, I did not think it probable that Christian, in the weak state the ship was in, would attempt to settle upon either of them, and as there was some plausibility in the infor-mation given me by Hillbrant the prisoner, and as the Duke of York's Island seemed to answer the description of such an is-land as Christian had been heard by others to declare he would search for to settle on, it being by Mr. Byron's account uninhab-ited, and with a harbour; and as the fact that it was out of the known track of ships in these seas since our acquaintance with the Society Islands, made it still more eligible for his purpose; from these united circumstances I thought it was probable he might make choice of the Duke of York's Island for his intended settlement. I therefore determined to proceed to that island, tak-ing Palmerston's island in my way thither, as it also answered in all respects, except situation, to the description of the other; and at night I bore away and made sail for Palmerston's Island, and made that on the 21st in the afternoon.[9]

On the 22nd in the morning sent the schooner tender and cutter in shore to look for the harbours or anchorage, and soon after Lieutenant Corner was sent in the yawl for the same pur-pose and to look out for the *Bounty* and her people. At noon, perceiving the schooner and cutter had got round the North-ernmost island, I stood round the S.E. island with the ship in or-der to join the yawl that was at a grapnel off that island, and sent

9. Discovered by Cook in his second voyage. There are nine small islands connected by a reef, covered with trees, but destitute of water.

the other yawl to join Lieutenant Corner. At 4 the two yawls returned with a quantity of cocoanuts and Lieutenant Corner also returned on board. Soon after, Lieutenant Hayward was sent on shore in the yawl to examine the S.W. island. After dark we burnt several false fires as signals to the boat, but the weather being thick and squally she did not return till the morning of the 23rd, but the tender joined us that night and informed me that she had found a yard on the island marked "*Bounty*'s Driver Yard" and other circumstances that indicated that the *Bounty* was, or had been there. The tender was immediately sent on shore after the yawl.

On the 23rd provisions, ammunition, &c., was sent on board the tender,[10] and Lieutenant Corner with a party of men were sent with the yawl and tender to land on the Northernmost island. At 4 in the afternoon, perceiving that the schooner tender had anchored under that island the yawl landing the party on the reef leading to it, Lieutenant Corner had orders to examine that and the Easternmost island very minutely to see if any other traces besides the yard could be made out of the *Bounty* or her people.

On the 24th in the morning sent the cutter on board the tender for intelligence, but she did not return till nearly 2 o'clock in the afternoon, when she brought with her seven men of Lieutenant Corner's party. She was sent on board the tender again with orders for the remainder of the party that was returned from the search to be brought on board the *Pandora* in the yawl, and for the cutter to remain on board the tender to embark Lieutenant Corner when he returned, the midshipman having represented that she answered the purpose of landing and embarking better than the larger boat from the particular circumstances of the landing place; and I stood over for the S.W. island to take on board the other yawl which had been sent to ground near the reef of that island and to procure from it some cocoanuts, &c.

---

10. Sufficient for thirty days at most. In the face of the danger of parting company, with the *Pandora* overloaded with stores, and the tender too feebly manned to wait at so dangerous a rendezvous as the Friendly Islands, Edwards showed very little foresight in neglecting to provision the tender for an independent voyage. His neglect nearly cost the crew their lives.

At 5 the yawl came on board, and I then stood towards the schooner in order to take the other yawl on board, but the weather became squally with rain and I stood out to sea. During the night the weather was rougher than usual, with an ugly sea and I did not get close in with them again till the 28th at noon, soon after which the yawl came on board from the schooner and informed us to my great astonishment and concern that the cutter had not been on board her since she left the ship. The tender was ordered to run down by the side of the reef and if the cutter was not seen there to run out to sea six leagues and to steer about W.N.W.-W., it being the opposite point to that on which the wind blew from the preceding night, and I waited with the ship to take on board Lieutenant Corner who was not then returned from the search. He soon after appeared and was taken on board.

In his search he found a double canoe curiously painted, and different in make from those we had seen on the islands we had visited. A piece of wood burnt half through was also found. The yard and these things lay upon the beach at high water mark and were all eaten by the sea worm, which is a strong presumption they were drifted there by the waves. The driver yard was probably drove from Toobouai where the *Bounty* lost the greater part of her spars, and as no recent traces could be found on the island of a human being or any part of the wreck of a ship I gave up all further search and hopes of finding the *Bounty* or her people there. I then stood out to sea and the ship and the tender cruised about in search of the cutter until the 29th in the morning, when seeing nothing of her, I being at that time well in with the land, sent on shore once more to examine the reef and beach of the northernmost island, but with no better success than before, as neither the cutter or any article belonging to her could be found there.

I then steered for the Duke of York's island which we got sight of at noon on the 6th June, and in the afternoon the tender and two yawls were sent on shore to examine the coast. On the 7th in the morning Lieutenant Corner and Hayward were sent on shore with a party of men attended by the schooner and two yawls. We soon after saw some huts upon the island and so made a signal to the boats to warn them of danger, and for them to be upon their guard against surprise. They landed and got canoes to the within side of the lagoon in which they made a circuit of it. A few houses were found in examining the hills on the opposite side of the lagoon, and also a ship's large wooden buoy, which appeared to be of foreign make, and had evident marks of its having been long in the water.

As Mr. Byron describes the Duke of York's island to be without inhabitants, the sight of the houses and ship's buoy, before they were minutely examined writ so strongly on the minds of the people that they saw many things in imagination that did not exist, but all tended to persuade them that the *Bounty's* people were really upon the island agreeable to the intelligence given by Hillbrant, but after a most minute and repeated search, no human being of any description could be found upon the island. There were a number of canoes, spare paddles, fishing gear, and a variety of other things found in the houses which seemed to prove that it was an occasional residence and fishery of the natives of some neighbouring islands.[11]

There is so great a difference in the situation of this island as laid down in the charts of Hawkesworth's collection of voyages and also some others from that of Captain Cook that there may be some doubt about its real situation. I followed that of Captain Cook, yet the situation of this island by our account did not exactly agree with him. He lays it down in Latitude 8° 41' S. and Longitude 173° 3' W., and the centre of the island by our account lies Latitude 8° 34' S. and Longitude by observation 172° 6', and by timekeeper 172° 39' W. By our estimation this island is not so large as it is by Mr. Byron's. In other respects, except the houses, it answers his description very well. I should have stood off to the westward to have seen if there were any other islands in that direction, but I was apprehensive by so doing that I might have much difficulty in fetching the island I had then to visit, and as the wind was favourable to stand to the Southward

---

11. Fakaafo or Bowditch Island, whence the present permanent inhabitants migrated.

when I left the island, I therefore satisfied myself in passing to the westward of it and stretching to the northward so far as to know there was no island within thirty miles of it on that point of the compass, and also to pass to the windward of the island when I put about and stood to the northward.

In standing to the Northward I discovered an island on the 12th June.[12] We soon perceived that it was a lagoon island, formed by a great many small islands connected together by a reef of rocks, forming a circle round the lagoon in its centre. It is low, but well wooded, amongst which the cocoanut tree is conspicuous both for its height and peculiar form. As we approached the land we saw several natives on the beach. Lieutenant Hayward was sent with the tender and yawl in shore to reconnoitre and to endeavour to converse with the natives, and if possible to bring about a friendly intercourse with them. They made signs of friendship and beckoned him to come on shore, yet, whenever he drew near with the boat, they always retired, and he could not prevail on them to come to her; and the surf was thought too great to venture to land, at least before the friendship of the natives was better confirmed.

We soon afterwards saw several sailing canoes with stages in their middle, sailing across the lagoon for the opposite islands, but whether it was a flight, or that they were only going a-fishing, or on some other business, we were at that time at a loss to know. Lieutenant Corner was sent to look for a better landing place, and, thinking that there was the appearance of an opening into the lagoon round the N.W. island, I stood that way with the ship to take a view of it but found that it was also barred in that part by a reef. Better landing places were found, but they were to leeward and at a considerable distance from the place that seemed to be the principal residence of the natives.

The next morning Lieutenant Corner and Hayward landed with a strong party near the houses, which they found deserted by the natives, and they had taken with them all the canoes ex-

---

12. Nukunono, a new discovery, another of the Union Group. It was surveyed by the American Exploring Expedition in 1840, and was found to be 7-2/10 miles long, N. and S., and 5 miles E. and W.

cept one. It appeared exactly to resemble those we had seen at the Duke of York's island. The houses, fishing gear and utensils were also similar to those seen there, which made me suppose that these were the people who occasionally visited that island, but this had the appearance of being the principal residence as Morais, or burying places, were found at this, but none at the former.

I was very desirous to get into communication with these people, as I thought we might possibly get some useful information relative to the buoy we had seen at the Duke of York's island, or about the *Bounty* had she touched at either of these islands, or at any others in their neighbourhood. With that view I left in and about the houses hatchets, knives, glasses and a variety of things that I thought would be useful or pleasing to them, and also to show them that we were disposed to be friendly to them, and by that means I hoped they would become less shy, and that our intercourse with them would be brought about; and I stood round the northernmost island to visit other parts of the island, and on the 14th in the morning Lieutenant Corner was sent on shore with the tender, yawl and canoe, and he landed to the eastward of the northernmost island and marched round to the northeast extremity of the islands: he perceived marks of bare feet of the natives in different parts, but more particularly about the cocoanut trees, most of which were stripped of their fruit, but not a single person or canoe could be found. He embarked again at that part of the isles with great difficulty by the assistance of cork jackets and rope and the canoe. I supposed that the natives had left the island and I bore away to join the tender that had been sent to search for a channel into the lagoon near the northernmost isle; and after joining her I went once more towards the place we had first examined, and seeing no natives or any signs of them there I gave up the search.

On the 15th stood to the southward for Navigators' islands. I called the island the Duke of Clarence's Island. It lies in Latitude 9° 9' 30" and Longitude 171° 30' 46".[13] From the abundance of cocoanut trees both on this and the Duke of York's Island, in the trunks of which holes were cut transversely to catch and pre-

13. The actual position is 9·5' S. Latitude and 171·38' W. Longitude.

serve water, and as no other water was seen by us we supposed it was the only means they had of procuring that useful and necessary article. On the 18th in the forenoon we saw a very high island and as I supposed it to be a new discovery I called it Chatham island,[14] and standing in for it, I perceived a Bay towards the N.E. end and I made a tack to endeavour to look into it. Perceiving that I could not accomplish my intentions before night I bore away and ran along the shore and sent the tender to reconnoitre, and found, opposite to a sandy beach where there was an Indian town, she got 25 fathoms about a quarter of a mile from the reef, which runs off the place and carries soundings of sand regularly in to 5 fathoms.

In the morning a boat was sent to ground in an opening in the reef before the town, in which 3 fathoms of water was found, and 2½ fathoms within it. This harbour is situated on the North side near the middle, but rather nearest to the West end.[15] We were told that there was a river there, and another or two between it and the South end. We then ran round the West to the S.W. end of the island and in the bay there 25 fathoms of water was found, the bottom rather foul and bad landing for a ship's boat. The natives said there was another, but the boat being called on board by signal she did not dare to examine into the truth of their report. We found here a native of the Friendly Islands, who called himself Fenow, and a relation of the chief of that name of Tongataboo.[16] Fenow said he had seen Captain Cook and English ships at the Friendly Islands, and that the natives of this island had never seen a ship before they saw the *Pandora*. The island is more than 30 miles long. A high mountain extends almost from one extremity to the other, which tapers down gradually at the ends and sides to the sea where it generally terminates in perpendicular cliffs of moderate height, except in a few places where there is a white beach of coral sand. The

14. Savaii in the Samoa Group. If not the 'Beauman' Islands seen by Roggewein in 1721, they were discovered by Bougainville in 1768 and visited by La Pérouse in 1787. Freycinet also visited them before Edwards.
15. Mata-atua Harbour. There is no river there except after heavy rain.
16. He had a finger cut off in mourning for Finau Ulukalala, who must have died in 1790.

natives called the island Otewhy;[17] latitude of Northernmost point 13° 27' 48" S. Longitude 172° 32' 13" W. South Point Latitude 13° 46' 18" S., Longitude 172° 18' 20" W., and East point in Latitude 13° 32' 20" S. and Longitude 172° 2' W.

On the 21st we saw another island[18] about 4 leagues to the Eastward of this, and there are two small islands between them, a small one in the middle and four off its East end, three of which are of considerable height. There is a greater variety of mountains and valleys in this than in Chatham's and it is exceedingly well wooded, and the trees of enormous size grow upon the very summits of the mountains with spreading heads resembling the oak. The same sort of trees were also seen in the same situation at Chatham, but not in so great abundance. This island is near forty miles long and of considerable breadth. The natives called it Oattooah.[19] Their canoes (although not so well finished), language and some of their customs much resemble those of the Friendly Islands, but they have some peculiar to themselves—that of dyeing their skins yellow and which is a mark of distinction amongst them is one of them.[20] The Latitude of the West point is 13° 52' 25" S. and Longitude 171° 49' 13" W. and the S.E. part in Latitude 14° 3' 30" S. and Longitude 171° 12' 50" W. As this island by our account was considerably to the Westward of the Navigators' islands, we at first supposed it to be a new discovery, but in visiting the other of the Navigators' islands discovered by Mons. Bougainville and running down again upon this we had reason to suppose that the S.E. end of Oattooah had been seen by him at a distance, and that it was the last island of the group that he saw.[21]

---

17. La Pérouse and Kotzebue call it Pola.
18. Upolu on which is Apia, the present capital of Samoa.
19. Upolu is the native name, but it has been called Ojalava, Oahtooha, Ojatava, and Opoloo by different navigators, who may have taken the names of villages or districts to mean the whole island. The population exceeded 20,000 at the beginning of last century.
20. Turmeric powder, never a mark of distinction, was besmeared over nursing mothers, chief women at the feasts connected with puberty, and persons concerned in certain other ceremonies.
21. Bougainville sighted Upolu on May 5th, 1760. A thick fog which came on that afternoon, and lasted all the following (continued on next page)

Between five and six o'clock of the evening of the 22nd June lost sight of our tender in a thick shower of rain. Some thought that they saw her light again at eight o'clock, but in the morning she was not to be seen. We cruised about for her in sight of the island on the 23rd and 24th and as I could not find the tender near the place where she was first lost, I thought it better to make the best of my way to Annamooka, the place appointed as a last rendezvous and to endeavour to get there before her, lest her small force should be a temptation to the natives to attack her, and accordingly we stood to the Southward. When we were to the Eastward of Oattooah we saw another island bearing from us about E.S.E. eight leagues. We afterwards knew that this was one of the Navigators' islands seen by Mons. Bougainville. On the morning of the 28th we saw the Happy Islands, and before noon a group of islands to the Eastward of Annamooka. We passed round to the Southward of these islands and ran down between little Annamooka and the Fallafagee isles and on the 29th anchored in Annamooka Road.

Whilst we were watering the ship, &c. I sent Lieutenant Hayward to the Happy Islands in a double canoe, which I hired of Tooboo a chief of these islands for the purpose of examining them and to make inquiries after the *Bounty* and the tender, but no intelligence could be got of either of these vessels at these two islands, nor at either of the Happy islands, and having completed our water and got a plentiful supply of yams and a few hogs, we sailed from thence on the 10th July. The natives were very daring in their thefts, but some of the articles stolen were recovered again by the chiefs, yet many of them were entirely lost, and as I did not think it proper to carry things to extremities on that occasion for fear that too much rigour might operate to the disadvantage of the tender should she arrive at the island in our absence, which I told them I expected she would do, and that I intended to return with the ship in about 20 days, and I

day, prevented him from approaching it, and from seeing Savaii, which he would have seen on May 7th in clear weather. La Pérouse coasted along its southern shore on December 17th, 1789. Unfortunately, smarting from the massacre of de Langle and his boat's crew at Tutuila, he was in no mood for communicating with the natives, and he did not anchor.

left a letter of instructions for the tender with Moukahkahlah, a resident chief, which he promised to deliver. He is not the superior chief, but we found him most useful to us and I thought him the most worthy of trust.

Whilst we were at Annamooka, Fattahfahe[22] the chief of all the islands, and who generally resides at Tongataboo or Amsterdam Island, came to visit us, as did also a great number of the chiefs from the adjacent islands and to all of whom I gave presents and also to such of their friends and attendances that were introduced for the purpose of receiving favours. A person called Toobou was the principal person in authority at Annamooka when we arrived there. I learned that he belonged to Tongataboo, and had little property on the island he governed, and I supposed that he was a deputy or minister of Fattahfahe who is generally acknowledged to be the superior chief of all the islands known under the names of the Friendly, Happy, and also of many other islands unknown to us. Fattahfahe and Toobou were on board the *Pandora* when she got under way, attended by two large double sailing canoes, the largest of which had upwards of 40 persons on board. I suppose that they came on board to take leave and in expectation of getting some additional farewell presents, in which they were not disappointed.

I knew that Fattahfahe was shortly going to make a tour of the Happy Islands, and as I perceived that he was exceedingly well pleased with what I had given him, and with his situation and accommodation on board the ship, I invited him to come with us to Toofoa and Kaho, two islands I was then steering for and that I intended to visit, as I thought he would be useful by procuring us a favourable landing at Toofoa, the island whose

22. Fatafehi is the hereditary title of one of the spiritual chiefs of Tonga. He had no executive authority, but his wealth, derived from his lands and the offerings to which he was entitled, gave him considerable influence. The complicated hierarchy of spiritual chiefs in Tonga was a continual puzzle to Cook. Fatafehi at this time was an ornamental personage, inferior in dignity to the Tui Tonga, and in power to Tukuaho, who wielded the authority of his father Mumui, the Tui Kanakubolu. The Toobou (Tubou) mentioned here was the deputy of the tyrant Tukuaho, who, eight years later, was to pay the penalty of his crimes in the Revolution of 1799. Hamilton mentions that the tradition of Tasman's visit in 1642 was still preserved.

inhabitants had behaved so treacherously to Lieutenant Bligh when he put in there for refreshments in the *Bounty*'s launch. Before the sun set we got within a small distance of the island, but it was too late for our boats to go on shore, and the canoes were sent to the islands to announce the arrival of these great chiefs; their coming in the ship I made no doubt would increase their consequence, and probably also the tribute they might think proper to impose on their subjects.

The next morning Lieutenant Corner, attended by the two chiefs, was sent on shore at Toofoa to search and to make the necessary inquiries after the *Bounty* and our tender, &c. and then to cross the channel which is about three or four miles over, and to do the same at Kaho, and when I saw the boat put off from Toofoa and stand over for the other island I bore away with the ship and ran through the channel between the two islands. At four in the afternoon Lieutenant Corner, Fattahfahe and Toobou, returned on board without success in their search and inquiries. The two chiefs were put on board their canoes, and they made sail for the Happy Islands.[23]

I now intended to have visited Tongataboo and the other of

23. Among the people who boarded the ship from Tofoa Lieutenant Hayward recognized some of those who attacked Bligh's boat four days after the mutiny, and murdered Quartermaster Norton, but solicitude for the crew of the tender, which might call there, prevented Edwards from punishing them as they deserved. No doubt, both at Tofoa and Namuka, the natives would have attempted to take the ship had they thought success possible as, we now know, they had planned to capture Cook's ships, and as they actually did capture the privateer *Port-au-Prince* in 1806 at Haapai. In 1808 William Mariner, one of the survivors of that ill-fated ship, who has left behind him the best account of a native race that exists probably in any language, was led by the strange native account of Norton's murder, to visit his grave. The natives asserted that Norton was killed by a carpenter for the sake of an axe which he was carrying; that his body was stripped and dragged some distance inland to a *Malae* where it lay exposed for three days before burial; and that the grass had never since grown upon the track of the body nor upon its resting-place on the *Malae*. Mariner found a bare track leading inland from the beach and terminating in a bare patch, lying transversely, about the length and breadth of a man. It did not appear to be a beaten path, nor were there people enough in the neighbourhood to make such a path. Probably it was an old track, long disused and forgotten, for by such natural causes is man's belief in the supernatural fed.

the Friendly Islands, but, as the wind was Southerly and unfavourable for the purpose, I took the resolution once more to visit Oattooah, and also the Navigators' Islands in search of the *Bounty* and our tender and to endeavour to fall in to the eastward of those islands. On the morning of the 12th we discovered a cluster of islands bearing from us W. by S. to N.W. by N., but as the wind was favourable for us to proceed I did not think it proper to lose time in examining them now, but intended to do it on my return to the Friendly Islands.[24]

On the 14th, in the forenoon, we saw three islands, which we supposed to be the three first islands seen by Mons. Bougainville and part of the cluster called by him "Navigators' Islands," the largest of these islands the natives called Toomahnuah.[25] We passed them at a convenient distance and several canoes came towards the ship, and it was with great difficulty that we prevailed on them to come alongside, and still greater difficulty to get them into the ship. They brought very few things in their canoes except cocoanuts, which I bought, and then gave them a few things as presents before they left the ship, and after making the necessary inquiries as far as our limited knowledge of the language would permit us, I proceeded to the Westward and before daylight on the morning of the 15th we saw another island. We ran down on the North side of it and brought to occasionally to find and take on board canoes.

We found the same shyness amongst the natives here as at the last islands, but a few presents being given to them they at last ventured on board. The island is called by them Otootooillah.[26] It is at least 5 leagues long; we supposed it to be another of the islands

24. The Vavau Group, called by the natives Haafuluhao, which then as now, owed spiritual allegiance to Tonga.
25. Manua, the most Easterly of the Samoa Group, called Opoun by La Pérouse.
26. Tutuila, discovered by Roggewein in 1721, visited by Bougainville 4th May, 1768, and by La Pérouse 10th December, 1787. On the day before his murder by the natives, Comte de Langle, La Pérouse's second in command, discovered Pangopango harbour while on a walk through the island, but neither Bougainville nor La Pérouse seems to have discerned the masked fissure in the cliff which forms its entrance. Edwards must have had a copy of Bougainville on board, but no record of La Pérouse's visit four years before, or he would have shown greater caution (continmued on next page)

seen by Mons. Bougainville. We got soundings in 53 fathoms water, and the depth decreased as we stood in shore, and there is probable anchorage on this side of the island sheltered from the prevailing winds, but we did not see the reef mentioned by Mons. Bougainville to run two leagues from the west end.

After making inquiries after the *Bounty* and tender and making presents to our visitors, we steered to the Westward, inclining to the North and before night saw Oattooa, bearing W.N.W. The South East end of this island was also probably seen by Mons. Bougainville, but by his description he could only have had a distant and a very imperfect view of the island. On the 16th we ran down on the South side of it, almost to the West end, and had frequent communication with the natives, but could get no information relative either to the *Bounty* or our tender. We saw a few of the natives with blue, mulberry and other coloured beads about their necks, and we understood that they got them from Cook at Tongataboo, one of the Friendly Islands. Having finished my business here, I stood to the Southward with the intention of visiting the group of islands we had discovered on our way hither, and we got sight of them again in the afternoon of the 18th.[27]

On the 19th, in the morning we ran down on the North side until we came to an opening through which we could see the sea on the opposite side, and a kind of sound is formed by some islands to the North East and some islands of considerable size to the South West, and in the intermediate space there are several small islands and rocks. On the larboard hand of the North entrance there is a shoal, on which the sea appears to break although there is from ten to twelve fathoms of water upon it. In the other part of the entrance there is forty fathoms of water or more. Our boat had only time to examine the entrance and the larboard side of the sound, in which there are interior bays where about 30 fathoms of water is to be found within a cables length of the shore. The branches of the sound on the starboard

in communicating with the natives. That he had heard something of La Pérouse's voyage, and had some ground for suspicion is shown by Hamilton. A detailed account of de Langle's murder is to be found in *La Pérouse's Voyage*, vol. ii.

27. Vavau.

side, and which are yet unexamined, appear to promise better anchorage than was found on the opposite shore, and should it turn out so, it will be by far the safest and best anchorage hitherto known amongst the Friendly Islands.[28]

The natives told us there was good water at several places within the sound, and there is plenty of wood. Several of the inferior chiefs were on board us, amongst whom were one of Fattahfahe's and one of Toobou's family, but the principal chief of the island was not on board, but we supposed he was coming at the time we made sail.[29] They brought on board yams, cocoanuts, some bread fruit, and a few hogs and fowls, and would have supplied us with more hogs had it been convenient for us to have made a longer stay with them, and which they entreated us much to do. We found them very fair in their dealings, very inoffensive and better behaved than any savages we had yet seen.

They have frequent communication with Annamooka and the other Friendly Islands, and their customs and language appear to be nearly the same. I called the whole group Howe's Islands. The islands on the larboard side of the North entrance I distinguished by the names of Barrington[30] and Sawyer, two to the starboard side with the names of Hotham[31] and Jarvis.[32] A high island a considerable way to the

28. He might have added "in the Pacific," for it is a magnificent land-locked harbour, a little narrow for sailing ships to beat out of in a southerly wind, but excellent for steamships.
29. This was Finau Ulukalala, one of the most notable men in Tongan history. He had just succeeded his elder brother, the Finau (Feenow) of Captain Cook's visit in 1777. On April 21st, 1799, he conspired against Tukuaho, the temporal sovereign of Tonga and assassinated him, plunging Tonga into a civil anarchy which lasted twenty years. He was Mariner's patron and protector until his death in 1809. "The great master of Greek drama," says a writer in the *Quarterly Review*, "could have desired no better elements than are to be found in the history of this remarkable man; his remorseless ambition and his natural affections—his contempt for the fables and ceremonies of his country when in prosperity—his patient submission to them when in distress—his strong intellects—his evil deeds—and the death which was believed to be inflicted on him in vengeance by the over-ruling divinities whom he defied."
30. Hunga.
31. Niuababu.
32. Falevai.

North West I called Gardener's island,[33] and another high island to the South West was called Bickerton's island.[34] There is a small high isle about four miles to the S.W. of this, and a small low island about five or six miles to the S.E. by E. of Gardener's Island,[35] and several islands to the S.E. of the islands forming the sound and too several small islands within it to which no names were given.

On the 20th at two in the morning, we passed within two miles of the small island that lies to the S.E. from Gardener's island, and soon after saw Gardener's island, on the N.W. side of which there appeared to be tolerable good landing on shingle beach, and a little to the right of this place, at the upper edge of the cliffs is a volcano, from which we observed the smoke issuing. There are recent marks of convulsion having happened in the island. Some parts of it appear to have fallen in, and other parts to be turned upside down. This part of the island is the most barren land we have seen in the country.[36] At nine o'clock thought we saw a large island bearing N. by W. and I made sail towards it, and as the weather was hazy we did not discover our mistake till near noon, when I hauled the wind to the Southward. On the 23rd saw an island from the masthead which I suppose was one of the Pylstaart

33. Fonua Lei (Land of Whales' teeth).
34. Laté.
35. Toku.
36. These islands had already been twice visited and named, and Cook, though he did not visit them, gives all their native names in his list of the islands composing the Friendly or Tonga Group. The honour of their discovery belongs to the Spanish pilot Maurelle, who sailed from Manila in 1781, without proper charts or instruments and almost without provisions for his long voyage to America. Reduced to desperate straits by famine, he sighted Fonua Lei, the northernmost of the Tonga Group, which he called Margoura, believing it to be one of the Solomon Islands. At Vavau he was liberally entertained by Bau or Poulaho, the Tui Tonga of Cook's visit four years before. La Pérouse passed close to the islands in December, 1787, but, consistent with his determination to hold no further intercourse with natives after the murder of M. de Langle, did not enter the harbour of Neiafu. Edwards had no account of either of these voyages. La Pérouse's journals were not published until 1797. Fonua Lei was again destroyed by an eruption in 1846. The inhabitants who had plantations on it were removed to Vavau just in time.

Islands.[37] On the 26th in the morning saw the island of Middleburgh and on the 27th ran in between Middleburgh, Eooa and Tongataboo.

Several canoes came on board us from the different islands. We were then within half a mile of the last, and equally near to the shoals of the second, but not so near to Middleburgh, yet we were near enough to see into English Road. At these islands we could neither see nor get any satisfactory information relative to the objects of our search. The natives brought in their canoes, yams, cocoanuts and a few small hogs, and I made no doubt that I should have been able to procure plenty of these articles had it been convenient for me to have stayed at these islands. The difficulty in getting in and out of the harbour and the indifferent quality of the water were alone sufficient objections against my stopping here. The road at Annamooka was more convenient for getting out and in, and the water, although not of the best quality, is reported to be better than that found at Amsterdam, and Annamooka being the place I had appointed as a rendezvous for the tender I did not hesitate in giving the preference to it, and accordingly made the best of my way thither, and we saw the Fallafagee islands (which lie near Annamooka) before dark, and also Toofoa, Kaho and Hoonga Tonga islands to the Westward, which are visible at a greater distance.

On the 28th July anchored in Annamooka Road. The person who now had the principal authority on the shore was a young chief whom we had not seen before. There was the same respect paid to him as was paid to Fattahfahe and to Toobou; neither of these chiefs nor Moukahkahlah were now in the islands, and the natives were now more daring in their thefts than ever, and would sometimes endeavour to take things by force, and robbed and stripped some of our people that were separated from the party. Lieutenant Corner, who commanded the watering and wooding parties on shore, received a blow on the head and was robbed of a curiosity he had bought and held in his hand, and

---

37. There is only one. It was so named by Tasman 1642. Maurelle called it Sola. But Edwards probably mistook the twin islets of Hunga Tonga and Hunga Haapai for Pylstaart.

with which the thief was making off. Lieutenant Corner shot the thief in the back, and he fell to the ground; at the same instant the natives attempted to take axes and a saw from the wooding party, and actually got off with two axes, one by force and the other by stealth, but they did not succeed in getting the saw. Two muskets were fired at the thieves, yet it was supposed that they were not hurt, but we are told that the other man died of his wound. One of the yawls was on shore at the time, and the long boat was landing near her with an empty cask. Lieutenant Corner drew the wooding and watering parties towards the boats and then began to load them with the wood that was cut.

A boat was sent from the ship to inquire the cause of the firing that was heard, but before she returned a canoe came from the shore to inform the principal chief (whom I had brought on board to dine with me) that one of the natives had been killed by our people. The chief was very much agitated at the information, and wanted to get out of the cabin windows into the canoe, but I would not suffer him to do it and told him I would go on shore with him myself in a little time in one of the ship's boats. Our boat soon returned and gave me an account of what had passed on shore. I told the chief that the lieutenant had been struck, and that he and his party had been robbed of several things, and that I was very glad that the thief had been shot, and that I should shoot every person who attempted to rob us, but that no other person except the thief should be hurt by us on that account. The axes and some other things that had been stolen before were returned and very few robbings of any consequence were attempted and discovered until the day of our departure.

I took this opportunity of showing the chief what execution the cannon and carronades would do by firing a six-pound shot on shore and an eighteen-pounder carronade loaded with grape shot into the sea. I afterwards went on shore with two boats and took with me the chief and his attendants, and before I returned on board again told him that I should send on shore the next morning for water and wood, and that I should also come on shore myself in the course of the day, all which he approved of and desired me to do, and accordingly the next morning, the

31st July the watering and wooding parties were sent on shore and carried on their business without interruption, and in the afternoon I went on shore myself and made a small present to the chief and to some other people.

On the 2nd August, having completed my water, &c. and thinking it time to return to England I did not think proper to wait any longer for the tender, but left instructions for her commander should she happen to arrive after my departure, and I sailed from Annamooka, attended by a number of chiefs and canoes belonging to those and the surrounding islands. After the ship was under way some of the natives had the address to get in at the cabin windows and stole out of the cabin some books and other things, and they had actually got into their canoes before they were discovered. The thieves were allowed to make their escape, but the canoes that had stolen these things were brought alongside and broke up for firewood. During this transaction the other natives carried on their traffic alongside with as much unconcern as if nothing had happened.

I made farewell presents to all the chiefs and to many others of different descriptions, and after hauling round Annamooka shoals, passed to the Eastward of Toofoa and Kaho, and in the morning saw Bickerton's island and the small island to the South-ward of it. On the 4th, in the evening, saw land bearing N.N.W. At first we took it to be Keppel's and Boscowen's islands, which I intended to visit, and by account was only a few miles to the Westward of them. As we approached the land we perceived that it was only one island, and as I supposed that it was a new discovery I called it Proby's island.[38] The hills, of which there

---

38. Niua-fo'ou (New Niua), discovered by W. Cornelis Schouten in the Dutch ship *Eendracht* (*Unity*) on May 14th, 1616, and named by him Good Hope Island. Twelve canoes came off, and some of them attempted to take the boat that he had sent ashore for water, but desisted on discharge of a volley which killed two men. He wrote: "The island was full of black cliffs, green on the top, and black, and was full of coco-trees and black earth. There was a large village, and several other houses on the seashore: the land was undulating, but not very high." No ship is known to have visited the island from 1614 to this visit in 1791. The cocoanuts grown here are the largest in the world, but the specimens planted in other islands do not appear to maintain their abnormal size. The (continued on next page)

are a great many of different heights and forms, are planted with cocoanuts and other trees, and the houses of a larger size than we had usually seen on the islands in these seas; were on the tops of hills of moderate height. We passed from S.E. end to the east, round to the north and N.W.

Landing appeared to be very indifferent until we came near the N.W., where the land formed itself into a kind of bay, and where the landing appeared to be better. The natives brought on board cocoanuts and plantains, all of which I bought, and made them a present of a few articles of iron. They told us that they had water, hogs, fowls and yams on shore and plenty of wood. They spoke nearly the same language as at the Friendly Islands. It lies in latitude 15° 53' S. and longitude 175° 51' W. I was now convinced that I was rather further to the Westward than I expected, and examining the island had carried me still further that way. I therefore gave up my intention of visiting Boscowen's and Keppel's islands,[39] as the regaining the Easting necessary would take up more time than would be prudent to allow at this advanced time of the season, and as soon as I had made the necessary inquiries, &c., after the *Bounty*, &c., our course was shaped with a view to fall in to the Eastward of Wallis' Island,[40] and the next day, the 5th, a little before noon saw that island bearing West by South, estimated by the master at ten leagues, but I did not myself suppose it to be more than seven leagues from us at that time.

---

island is further remarkable from the fact that the Megapodius, or Scrub hen, is plentiful there, and nowhere else in the Pacific further east than the New Hebrides. The natives have no traditions of its introduction. The eggs have been prized as a delicacy in Tonga for centuries, and are exported thither by every canoe going southward during the breeding season. It is said that they are sometimes hatched artificially, but the young *malao* does not take kindly to the bush in Tonga, although the vegetation is much the same. Why should the bird be found in Polynesia, having skipped all the intermediate islands of Melanesia? To what story of the migration of races is it the only clue?

39. Niuatobutabu, like Niuafoou, subject to the King of Tonga.
40. Uea, discovered by Wallis in 1767, and visited by Maurelle on April 22nd, 1781. It has 3000 inhabitants who are said by the French missionaries to be increasing. Uea is nominally independent under its own queen, but the French priests wield the real power in so spirited a fashion that the natives frequently attempt to escape from the island as stowaways.

Canoes came off to us and brought us cocoanuts and fish, which they sold for nails, and I also made them a present of some small articles which I always made a rule to do to first adventurers, hoping that it might turn out advantageous to future visitors, but they went away before I had given them all I intended. They told us that there was running water, hogs and fowls on shore. They spoke the language of the Friendly Islands, and I observed that one of the men had both of his little fingers cut off, and the flesh over his cheekbones very much bruised after the manner of the natives of those islands.[41]

In the evening I bore away and made sail to the Westward intending to run between Espiritu Santo and Santa Cruz, and to keep between the tracks of Captain Carteret and Lieutenant Bligh, and on the 8th at 10 at night saw land bearing from the W. by S. We had no ground at 110 fathoms. At daylight I bore away and passed round the East end and ran down on the South side of the island. There is a white beach on these parts of the island on which there appears to be tolerable good landing, or better than is usually seen on the islands in these seas, and there is probably anchorage in different places on this side or under the small islands, of which there are several near the principal island, but as I did not hoist out the boats to sound that still remains a doubt.

There are cocoanut trees all along the shore behind the beach, and an uncommon number of boughs amongst them. The island is rather high, diversified with hills of different forms, some of which might obtain the name of mountain, but they are cultivated up to their very summits with cocoanut trees and other articles, and the island is in general as well or better cultivated and its inhabitants more numerous for its size than any of the islands we have hitherto seen. The principal island is about 7 miles long and three or four broad, but including the islands off its East and West ends, and which latter are joined to it by a reef, it is about ten miles long. I called it Grenville Island, supposing it to be a new discovery. Its latitude is 12° 29' and longitude 183° 03'W.

A great number of paddling canoes came off and viewed the ship at a distance, and I believed that their intentions were

41. Mourning for the death of a chief or near relation.

at first hostile. They were all armed with clubs and they had a great quantity of stones in their canoes which they use in battle, and they all occasionally joined in a kind of war-whoop. We made signs of peace, and offered them a variety of toys which drew them alongside, and then into the ship where they behaved very quietly; probably the unexpected presents they got from us, and our number and strength might operate in favour of peace. However, they seemed to have the same propensity to thieving as the natives of the other islands, and gave us many, some of which ludicrous, examples.

Although at so great a distance they said that they were acquainted with the Friendly islands, and had learned from them the use of iron.[42] They were tattooed in a different manner from the natives of the other islands we had visited, having the figure of a fish, birds and a variety of other things marked upon their arms. Their canoes were not so delicately formed nor so well finished as at the Friendly islands, but more resemble those of the Duke of York's, the Duke of Clarence's and the Navigators' islands. Neither sailing or double canoes came on board, neither did we see any of either of these descriptions. They told us that water and many other useful things, the usual produce of the islands in these seas, could be procured on shore.

Their language appeared something to resemble that spoken at the Friendly islands, and after asking them such questions as we thought necessary, some of which probably were not understood

42. This confirms the story of Kau Moala, a Tongan navigator, who returned to his native land in 1807 and related his adventures to Mariner. He had visited Futuna, Rotuma and Fiji in a double canoe, and, in describing Rotuma, he related the legend of two giants who had migrated from Tonga to Rotuma in legendary times. He was shown gigantic bones in proof of the story, the bones, no doubt, of some marine monster. Mention is made of Rotuma in a Tongan saga of the early sixteenth century, and there can be no doubt that there was occasional intercourse between these distant islands during the period when the Tongans were the Norsemen of the Pacific. Kau Moala heard nothing of Edwards' visit, though he brought news of the visit of a ship to Futuna, and of an ineffectual attempt to take her—perhaps the visit of Schouten, whose account of the affray tallies closely with theirs even to the killing of six natives. The tradition was still fresh after 190 years. Edwards' visit, having brought no disasters on the natives, escaped the attention of the native poets and was forgotten.

perfectly by them, or their answers by us, we made sail and continued our course to the Westward. No women were seen in the canoes that visited us, which curiosity or the hope of getting some pleasing toys usually bring to our side, but this is another proof that their original intentions were hostile. We passed the island in so short a time that those who neglected to come out at our first appearance had not afterwards the opportunity to visit us.

On the 11th at eleven o'clock in the morning we struck soundings on a bank in twelve to fourteen fathoms water and at ten minutes after eleven had no ground in one hundred and forty fathoms. No land was then in sight, nor did we get any soundings after in the course of the day. It was called *Pandora's* Bank, its Latitude 12° 11' S. and Longitude 188° 68' W.

On the next morning saw a small island which met in two high hummocks and a steeple rock which lies high on the West side of the hummocks. It obtained the name of Mitre Island. The shore appeared to be steep to, and we had no bottom at 120 fathoms within three quarters of a mile of the shore. There was no landing place or sign of inhabitants. The tops of the hills were covered with wood. There was also some on the sides, but not in so great an abundance they being too steep and too bare of soil in some places to support it. Latitude 11° 49' S. and Longitude 190° 04' 30" W.[43]

By nine o'clock we had passed it and steered to the Westward, and soon afterwards we saw another island bearing N.W. by N. We hauled up to the N.W. to make it out more distinctly as it is of considerable height, yet not much more than a mile long, and the top and the side of the hills very well cultivated and a number of houses were seen near the beach in a bay on the South side of the island. The beach from the East round to the South of the West end is of white sand, but there was then too much surf for the ship's boat to land upon it with safety. I called it Cherry's Island. Its Latitude is 11° 37' S. and Longitude 190° 19' 30" W.[44]

---

43. Native name Fataka. The Russian Captain Kroutcheff, who landed upon it in 1822, found it uninhabited.
44. Kroutcheff placed it 41 minutes further west.

On the 13th August a little before noon we saw an island bearing about N.W. by N. In general it is high, but to the West and North West the mountain tapered down to a round point of moderate height. It abounds with wood, even the summits of the mountain are covered with trees. In the S.E. end there was the appearance of a harbour, and from that place the reef runs along the South side to the Westernmost extremity. In some places its distance is not much more than a mile from the shore, in other places it is considerably more. Although we were sometimes within less than a mile of the reef we saw neither house nor people. The haziness of the weather prevented us from seeing objects distinctly, yet we saw smoke very plain, from which it may be presumed that the island is inhabited. It is six or seven leagues long and of considerable breadth. I called it Pitt's Island. Its Latitude is 11° 50' 30" S. South point, and Longitude 193° 14' 15" W.[45]

At midnight between the 16th and 17th of August breakers were discovered ahead and upon our bow, and not a mile from

---

45. This was Vanikoro in the Santa Cruz Group. It was probably seen by Mendaña in 1595, and again by Carteret in 1767, but the interest attached to it by Europeans, and particularly to Edwards' visit, lies in the undoubted fact that at that very time there were survivors of La Pérouse's ill-fated expedition upon it. If his search for the mutineers had been as keen at this part of his voyage as it was in the earlier portion, he would have been the means of rescuing them. The smoke he saw may well have been signal fires lighted by the castaways to attract his attention. La Pérouse's ships were cast away in 1788, just three years before, shortly after the Commander had delivered his journals to Governor Phillip in Botany Bay for transmission to Europe. Their fate was unknown until Peter Dillon chanced upon a French sword hilt in Tucopia thirty-eight years later in 1826. Satisfying himself that they had been brought from Vanikoro, he persuaded the East India Company to place him in command of a search expedition. In 1827 he made a thorough examination of the island, and found the remains of the *Boussole*; the *Astrolabe*, according to the native account, having foundered in deep water. He found the clearing where the survivors had felled timber to build themselves a brig in which they sailed to meet a second shipwreck elsewhere, perhaps on the Great Barrier reef of Queensland. But two had been left, and of these one had died shortly before his visit, and the other had gone with the natives to another island leaving no trace behind him. D'Entrecasteaux, when in search of La Pérouse in 1793, also passed within sight of the castaways. D'Urville made a thorough examination of the island both in 1828 and 1838. The relics brought home by Dillon may be seen in the Gallerie de la Marine in the Louvre.

us. We were lying to and heaving the lead at the time and had no ground at 120 fathoms. We wore the ship and stood from them and in less than an hour after more breakers were seen extending more than a point before our lee beam, but we made more sail and so got clear of them all. At daylight we put about with the intention of examining the breakers we had seen in the night and we made two boards, but perceiving that I could not weather them without some risk I bore up and ran round its N.W. end. It is a double reef enclosing a space of deeper water like the lagoon islands so common in these seas, and probably will become one in the course of time. The sea breaks pretty high upon it in different parts, but there is no part of the reef absolutely above water. It is about seven miles long in the direction of N.W. by N. Its breadth is not so much. Called it Willis's shoal. It lies in Latitude 12° 20' S. and Longitude 200° 2' W.[46]

We pursued our course to the Westward and on the 23rd saw the land bearing from N.E. to N. by W. The Easternmost land when first seen was ten or twelve leagues from us and it cannot be far to the Westward of the land seen by Mons. Bougainville and called by him Louisiade, and probably joins to it. The cape is in Latitude 10° 3' 32" S. and Longitude 212° 14' W., was called Cape Rodney and another cape in Latitude 9° 58' S. and Longitude 212° 37' W. was called Cape Hood, and an island lying between them was called Mount Clarence. After passing Cape Hood the land appears lower and to branch off about N.N.W. and to form a deep and wide bay, or perhaps a passage through, for we saw no other land, and there are doubts whether it joins New Guinea or not.[47]

---

46. This was the dangerous reef now known as Indispensable Reef, after the ship *Indispensable* commanded by Captain Wilkinson, who discovered it in 1790.
47. It was, in fact, the mainland of New Guinea. The land East of Cape Rodney, comprising Orangerie, Table, and Cloudy Bays, lies so low and is so generally obscured with haze that on a dull day Edwards would not have seen it. It is doubtful whether Edwards' Capes Rodney and Hood, are correctly placed in the modern charts. Our Cape Rodney is not a conspicuous headland, and it lies half a degree eastward of 212·14 W. Longitude, and 9' South of 10^{6}·3° S. Latitude. Edwards' positions are usually so accurate that I cannot see why they should have been departed from. Our Cape Hood, on the other hand, is exactly in the position of his Cape Rodney, and is besides a very conspicuous (continued on next page)

I pursued my course to the Westward between the Latitudes of 10° and 9° 33' S. keeping the mouth of Endeavour Straits open, by which I hoped to avoid the difficulties and dangers experienced by Captain Cook in his passage through the reef in a higher latitude, and also the difficulties he met with when within in his run from thence to the Strait's mouth.[48]

On the 25th August at 9 in the morning, saw breakers from the mast head bearing from us W. by S. to W.N.W. I hauled up to the Southward and passed to the Eastward of them. It runs in the direction of W.S.W. and E.N.E. 4' or 5', and another side runs in the direction of N.W. the distance unknown. The sea broke very moderately upon it, in some places barely perceptibly. In the interior part a very small sandbank was seen from the mast-head, and no other part of the reef was above water. It obtained the name of Look-Out Shoal.[49]

Before noon we saw more breakers which proved to be one of those half-formed islands enclosing a lagoon, the reef of which was composed principally of very large stones, but a sandbank was seen from the mast head extending to the Southward of it, and as I could not weather it and seeing another opening to the Westward, I steered to the W.S.W., and a little before two o'clock saw the island to the Westward of us, and another reef bearing about S.W. by South and I then steered W. ½ N. until

---

wooded tongue of land. Beyond is another conspicuous point. Round Head, which corresponds in position with Edwards' Cape Hood. Mount Clarence, moreover, would not appear to lie between Capes Rodney and Hood until the former was out of sight astern. I think that Mount Clarence must have been hidden by clouds, and that Edwards' Mount Clarence was in reality the high cone in the Saroa district, which is a conspicuous feature on the coast line. A further indication that the day was hazy lies in the fact that Edwards did not see the great Owen Stanley Range which towers up 13,000 feet behind. Had he done so he would not have mistaken the mainland for a group of scattered islands. Hamilton does not call Mount Clarence an "island," but a "mountain." A further proof that Edwards' "Cape Hood" was Round Head is found in the remark "After passing Cape Hood the land appears lower, and to branch off about N.N.W., . . . for we saw no other land." This applies to Round Head, and to no other part of the coast.
48. If he had kept this course he would have struck the New Guinea Coast again a little East of the Maikasa River.
49. East Bay.

half past five, when a reef was seen extending from the island a considerable way to the N.W., the island bearing then about W.S.W. I immediately hauled upon the wind in order to pass to the Southward of it, and seeing a passage to the Northward obstructed[50] I stood on and off, and was still during the night, and in the morning bore away; but as we drew near we also saw a reef extending to the Southward from the South end of the island. I ran to the Southward along the reef with the intention and expectation of getting round it, and the whole day was spent without succeeding in my purpose and without seeing the end of the reef, or any break in it that gave the least hopes of a channel fit for a ship.[51]

The islands, which I called Murray's Islands, are four in number, two of them are of considerable height and may be seen twelve leagues. The principal island is not more than three miles long. It is well wooded and at the top of the highest hill the rocks have the appearance of a fortified garrison. The other high island is only a single mountain almost destitute of trees and verdure. The other two are only crazy barren rocks. We saw three two mast boats under sail near the reef, which we supposed belong to the islands. Murray Islands lie in Latitude 9° 57' S. and Longitude 216° 43' W. We kept turning to the Southward along the reef until the 28th in search of a channel and in the forenoon of that day we thought we saw an opening through the reef near a white sandy island or key, and a little before Lieutenant Corner was sent in the yawl to examine it. At three quarters past four he made the signal that there was a channel through the reef fit for a ship, and after a signal was made and repeated for the boat to return on board, and after dark false fires and muskets were fired from the ship,

---

50. It is difficult to understand how Edwards failed to see Flinders Passage, which, while not free from obstructions to the westward, would have admitted him to a safe anchorage at the Murray Islands, inside the Barrier Reef.
51. It was an unfortunate choice. Had he steered north on first encountering the reefs he would have made the coast which he might have followed in safety, as Bligh did in his boat voyage after the mutiny, by what is now known as the Great North-East Channel. He was led Southward by his plan of using the Endeavour Straits. See Hamilton's account, pp. 141-2.

and answered with muskets by the boat repeatedly to point out the situation of each other. We sounded frequently but had no ground at 110 fathoms.

At about twenty minutes after seven the boat was seen close in under our stern and at the same time we got soundings in 50 fathoms water. We immediately made sail, but before the tacks were on board and the sails trimmed the ship struck upon the reef when we were getting 4¼ less 2 fathoms water on the larboard side, and 3 fathoms on the starboard side. Got out the boats with a view to carrying out an anchor, but before it could be effected the ship struck so heavily on the reef that the carpenters reported that she made 18 inches of water in five minutes, and in five minutes after there was four feet of water in the hold. Finding the leak increase so fast found it necessary to turn all hands to the pumps and to bale at the different hatchways. She still continued to gain upon us so much that under an hour and a half after she had struck there was eight feet of water in the hold, and we perceived that the ship had beat over the reef where we had 10 fathoms water. We let go the small bower and veered away the cable and let go the best bower under foot in 15 fathoms water to steady the ship. At this time the water only gained upon us in a small degree and we flattered ourselves for some time that by the assistance of a top sail which we were preparing and intended to haul under the ship's bottom we might be able to free her of water, but these flattering hopes did not continue long, for as she settled in the water the leaks increased and in so great a degree that there was reason to apprehend that she would sink before daylight.

In the course of the night two of the pumps were for some time rendered useless, one, however was repaired, and we continued baling and pumping the remainder of the night and every effort was made to keep her afloat.[52] Daylight fortunate-

---

52. Two men were crushed to death; one by a gun that had broken loose, and the other by a falling spar. The whole ship's company seems to have behaved splendidly, working at the pumps and at the sail they were preparing to haul under the ship's bottom until they could scarcely stand for fatigue, with nothing to replenish their strength but "a cask of excellent strong ale which we brewed at Anamooka" (Hamilton).

ly appeared and gave us the opportunity to see our situation and the surrounding danger. Our boats were kept astern of the ship; a small quantity of provisions and other necessaries were put into them, rafts were made, and all floating things upon the deck were unlashed. At half past six the hold was filled with water, and water was between decks and it also washed in at the upper deck ports, and there were strong indications that the ship was upon the very point of sinking, and we began to leap overboard and to take to the boats, and before everybody could get out of her the ship actually sank.[53] The boats con-

---

53. Every reader must be struck by the fact that in his description of this disaster, Edwards never once speaks of the prisoners. Hamilton, it is true, does say "The prisoners were ordered to be let out of irons," but another account, ascribed to Lieutenant Corner, second lieutenant of the *Pandora*, throws a sinister light on this part of the narrative. "Three of the *Bounty*'s people, Coleman, Norman, and M'Intosh, were now let out of irons, and sent to work at the pumps. The others offered their assistance, and begged to be allowed a chance of saving their lives; instead of which, two additional sentinels were placed over them, with orders to shoot any who should attempt to get rid of their fetters. Seeing no prospect of escape, they betook themselves to prayer, and prepared to meet their fate, everyone expecting that the ship would soon go to pieces, her rudder and part of the sternpost being already beat away. No notice was taken of the prisoners, as is falsely stated by the author of the *Pandora's Voyage*, although Captain Edwards was entreated by Mr. Heywood to have mercy upon them, when he passed over their prison to make his own escape, the ship then lying on her broadside, with the larboard bow completely under water. Fortunately the master-at-arms, either by accident or design, when slipping from the roof of 'Pandora's Box' into the sea, let the keys of the irons fall through the scuttle or entrance, which he had just before opened, and thus enabled them to commence their own liberation, in which they were generously assisted, at the imminent risk of his own life, by William Moulter, a boatswain's mate who clung to the coamings, and pulled the long bars through the shackles, saying he would set them free, or go to the bottom with them. Scarcely was this effected when the ship went down. The master-at-arms and all the sentinels sunk to rise no more. Among the drowned were Mr. Stewart, John Sumner, Richard Skinner, and Henry Hillbrandt, the whole of whom perished with their hands still in manacles." Some allowance is to be made both for the confusion of a shipwreck, and for the natural fear of the commander that in the loosening of the ties of authority natural to such a moment, the liberation among his crew of a number of men who had already mutinied successfully, and were going home with a rope about their necks, would be an act of merciful folly. This, however, does (continued on next page)

tinued astern on the ship in the direction of the drift of the tide from here, and took up the people that had held on to the rafts or other floating things that had been cast loose for the purpose of supporting them in the water.[54]

We loaded two of the boats with people and sent them to the island, or rather key, about three or four miles from the ship, and then other two boats remained near the ship for some time and picked up all the people that could be seen and then followed the two first boats to the key, and after landing the people, &c. the boats were immediately sent again to look about the wreck and the adjoining reefs for missing people, but they returned without having found a single person. On mustering we discovered that 89 of the ship's company and 10 of the pirates that were on board were saved, and that 31[55] of the ship's company and 4 pirates were lost with the ship. The boats were hauled up and secured to fit them for the intended run to Timor; an account was taken of the provision and other articles saved, and they were spread to dry, and we put ourselves to the following allowance, to 3 ounces of bread, which was occasionally reduced to 2 ounces, to half an ounce of portable soup, to half an ounce of essence of malt, (but these two articles were not served until after we left the key, and they were at other times withheld), to two small glasses of water and one of wine.

On the afternoon of the 30th sent a boat to the wreck to see if anything could be procured. She returned with the head of the T.G. mast, a little of the T.G. rigging, and part of the chain of the lightning conductor, but without a single article of provi-

---

not excuse him for refusing his prisoners the shelter of an old sail on the sand cay, and so obliging them to get shelter from the sun by burying themselves neck-deep in the sand, as Heywood afterwards stated. Heywood further asserted that after the vessel struck the prisoners, having wrenched themselves out of their irons, implored Edwards to let them out of "Pandora's Box," but that he had them all ironed again.

54. In his evidence before the court-martial Edwards said: "The double canoe, that was able to support a considerable number of men, broke adrift with only one man, and was bulged upon a reef, and afforded us no help when she was so much wanted."

55. Hamilton says 34.

sion. The boat was also sent to examine the channel through the reef &c. and was afterwards sent a-fishing. She lost her grapnel, but no fish were caught.

On the 31st the boats were completed and were launched, and we put everything we had saved on board of them and at half past ten in the forenoon we embarked, 30 on board the launch, 25 in the pinnace, 23 in one yawl and 21 in the other yawl.[56] We steered N.W. by W. and W.N.W. within the reef. This channel through the reef is better than any hitherto known, besides the advantage it has of being situated further to the North, by which many difficulties would be avoided when within the reef. In the run from thence to the entrance of Endeavour Straits there is a small white island or key on the larboard end of the channel, which lies in Latitude 11° 23' S., the sides are strong and irregular.

On the 1st September in the morning saw land, which probably was the continent of New South Wales. The yawls were sent on shore to ground and look out. They saw a run of water, landed and filled their two *barricois*, which were the only vessels of consequence they had with them, and I steered for an island called by Lieutenant Bligh Mountainous Island, and when joined by the boats ran into a bay of that island where we saw Indians on the beach. The water was shoal and the Indians waded off to the boats. I gave them some presents and made them sensible that we were in want of water. They brought us a vessel filled with water which we had given them for the purpose, and they returned to fill it again. They used many signs to signify that they wished us to land, but we declined their invitation from motives of prudence.

---

56. Each boat was supplied with the latitude and longitude of Timor, 1100 miles distant. As soon as they embarked the oars were laid athwart the boat so that they could stow two tiers of men. The men were distributed as follows: pinnace—Captain Edwards; Lieutenant Hayward; Rickards, master's mate; Packer, gunner; Edmonds, captain's clerk; 3 prisoners, 16 privates. Red yawl—Lieutenant Larkan; Surgeon Hamilton; Reynolds, master's mate; Matson, midshipman; 2 prisoners; 18 privates. Launch—Lieutenant Corner; Bentham, purser; Montgomery; carpenter, Bowling, master's mate; Mackendrick, midshipman; 2 prisoners; 24 privates. Blue yawl—George Passmore, master; Cunningham, boatswain; Innes, surgeon's mate; Fenwick, midshipman; Pycroft, midshipman; 3 prisoners; 15 privates.

Just as a person was entering the water with the second vessel of fresh water, an arrow was discharged at us by another person, which struck my boat on the quarter, and perceiving that they were collecting bows and arrows a volley of small arms was fired at them which put them to flight. I did not think proper to land and get water by force as land was seen at that time in different directions, which by appearance was likely to produce that article, and which I flattered myself we might be able to procure without being drove to that extremity. I therefore ran close along the shore of this island and landed at different places at some distance from the former situation. I also landed at another island near it which I called Plum Island[57] from its producing a species of that fruit, but we were unsuccessful in finding the article we were in search of, and in so much want of.

In the evening we steered for the islands which we supposed were those called by Captain Cook the Prince of Wales' Islands, and before midnight came to a grapnel with the boats near one of these islands, in a large sound formed by several of the surrounding islands, to several of which we gave names, and called the sound Sandwich Sound.[58] It is fit for the reception of ships, having from five to seven fathoms of water. There is plenty of wood on most of the islands, and by digging we found very good water. On the flat part of a large island which I called Lafory's Island,[59] situated on the larboard hand as we entered the sound from the Eastward we saw a burying place and several wolves[60] near the watering place, but we saw no natives. Here we filled our vessels with water and made two canvas bags in which we also put water, but with this assistance we had barely the means to take a gallon of water for each man in the boats. We sent our kettles on shore and made tea and portable broth, and a few oysters were picked off the rocks

57. Tree Island.
58. Now called Prince of Wales' Channel or Flinders Channel. It is the best Channel through Torres Straits, and, if Edwards' narrative had been published his discovery would doubtless have been perpetuated in his name.
59. Horn Island.
60. Dingoes.

with which we made a comfortable meal, indeed the only one we had made since the day before we left the ship.

On the 2nd September at half past three in the afternoon we stood out of the North entrance of the sound. Before five we saw a reef extending from the North to the W.N.W. and which appeared to run in the latter direction or more to the West-ward.[61] On the edge of this reef we had 3¼ fathoms of water and after hauling to the S.W. we soon deepened our water to 5 fathoms. Besides Mountainous and West Islands seen by Lieu-tenant Bligh we saw several other islands between the North and the West, one of which I called Hawkesbury Island. We saw several large turtle. In the evening we saw the Northernmost extremity of New South Wales, which forms the South side of Endeavour Straits. At night the boats took each other in tow and we steered to the westward.

It is unnecessary to retail our particular sufferings in the boats during our run to Timor and it is sufficient to observe that we suffered more from heat and thirst than from hunger, and that our strength was greatly decreased.[62] We fortunately had good weather, and the sea was generally not very rough, and the boats were more buoyant and lively in the water that we reasonably could have expected considering the weight and numbers we had in them.

At seven o'clock in the morning of the 13th September we saw the island of Timor bearing N.W. We continued our course to the W.N.W. till noon, but the other boats hauled for the land and we separated from them. At one o'clock we were well in with the land and a party was sent on shore in search of water, but none was found here, nor at several other places we examined as we passed along the coast, until the next morning, when good water was found. We also bought a few small fish, which when divided afforded some two or three ounces per

61. North West Reef.
62. Like Bligh's men, they wetted their shirts in salt water to cool them-selves by evaporation, but found that the absorption through the skin tainted the fluids of the body with salt so that the saliva became intolerable in the mouth. The young bore the want of water better than the old, but all alike became excessively irritable.

man. Here the launch joined us again. They informed us that they had got a supply of water the evening before.

On the 15th in the morning saw the island of Rotte. At half past three in the afternoon entered the Straits of Samoa. Before midnight we came to a grapnel off the float or Coopang and found here one ship, a ketch and two or three small craft. The launch separated from us soon after dark to get up to Coopang the next day in the forenoon. On the morning of the 16th by our account (which was the 17th in this country) at daylight we hailed the fort and informed them whom we were. A small boat was sent to us, and myself and Lieutenant Hayward landed at the usual place near the Chinese temple where we were received by the lieutenant governor, Mr. Fruy and Mr. Bouberg, captain lieutenant of a company ship that lay in the road, and conducted by them to Governor Wanjon, who received us with great humanity and goodness of heart. Refreshments were immediately prepared for myself and the lieutenant. Provision was provided, the people ordered to land, and they all dined in the Governor's own house, and an arrangement was made for the reception and accommodation of the whole party as they arrived.

The church and the church-yard was assigned for the use of the private seamen, a house was hired for the warrant and petty officers. The people that were ill were put under the care of Mr. Zimers, the Surgeon-General. Governor Wanjon did me and Lieutenant Hayward the honour of lodging and entertaining us in his own house. Mr. Corner, the second lieutenant and Mr. Bentham, the Purser, were received in the house of Mr. Fruy, the lieutenant-governor. Lieutenant Larkin and Mr. Passmore were taken into the house of Mr. Brouberg, the captain-lieutenant of the company ship, and Mr. Hamilton, the surgeon, was accommodated in the house of Mr. Zimers, the Surgeon-General, and Governor Wanjon did everything in his power to supply our present wants, or that would contribute to the re-establishment of our health and strength and even to our amusement, and this benevolent example was followed by Mr. Fruy, the lieutenant-governor and the other gentlemen of the place. Two months' provision was provided for the ship's company and put on board the *Remberg* (*Rembang*), a Dutch East India Company ship, and we embarked on board the same ship for Batavia on the 6th October, 1791.[63]

Before we sailed Governor Wanjon delivered to me eight men, one woman and two children who came to Coopang in June last in a six-oared cutter. They are supposed to be late deserters from the colony at Port Jackson. Food bills were given on the different departments of the Navy for the provisions and other necessaries we were supplied with at Coopang and also for the maintenance and clothing of the convicts. I sold one of the yawls to the lieutenant-governor and the longboat and the other yawl to the Commander of the *Remberg*, the ship in which we embarked. The latter was not to be delivered up until I left Batavia, and I shall make myself accountable to the Commissioners of His Majesty's Navy for the amount. As I could take no more boats with me and the pinnace being out of repair, I left her with the Governor Wanjon with permission to do with her what he thought proper.

We stopped at Samarang, being an island of Java, where we had the good fortune to be joined by our tender that had separated from us off the island of Oattoah. She had all her people on board except one man, whom they had buried a few days before. She had been stopped at Java on suspicion, and they were going to send her to Batavia. Mr. Overstratin, the Governor of the place, delivered her up to me. The tender had contracted a small debt for provisions &c. at Java, which I shall discharge. She fell in to the westward of Annamooka, the island I had ap-

---

63. This hospitality was not extended to the prisoners, who were confined in irons in the castle, and fed on bad provisions. But on the passage to Batavia in the *Rembang* they had worse in store, for the ship was partially dismasted in a cyclone, and would certainly have gone ashore but for the exertions of the English passengers. The prisoners took their turn at the pumps with the rest, and when their strength gave out, they were put in irons and allowed to rest upon a wet sail soaked with the drainings of a pigsty under which it was spread. At Batavia Edwards distributed the purchase-money of the tender among his people to enable them to buy clothes, and the prisoners, having their hands at liberty, made suits and hats for the *Pandora*'s crew, and so were able to buy clothes of their own.

pointed to rendezvous on, without seeing it, and then steered two days to the Westward nearly in its latitude and fell in with an island which I suppose must be one of the Fiji Islands, where they had waited for me five weeks, and then proceeded through Endeavour Straits and intended to stop at Batavia. With the iron and salt I had provided them with they were enabled to procure and preserve sufficient provision for their run to Java.

I arrived at Batavia on the 7th November and on application to the Governor and Council my people were put on board a Dutch East India Company's ship that was lying in the Road to be kept there until they could be sent to Europe, and the sick were ordered to be received by the company's hospital at Batavia, and I have since agreed with the Dutch East India Company to divide my ship's company into four parts, and to embark them on board four of their ships for Holland at no expense to the Government further than for the officers and prisoners, which appeared to me to be the most eligible and least expensive way of getting to England. Lieutenant Larkin, two petty officers, and eighteen seamen embarked on the *Zwan*, a Dutch East India ship on the 19th November and are sailing for Europe, and myself and the remainder of the *Pandora*'s company and the prisoners are to embark as soon as their ships are manned. Myself and the pirates are to embark on board the *Vreedenberg*, Captain Christian and I have stipulated that myself and the prisoners may be at liberty to go on board any of His Majesty's ships, or other vessels we may meet with on mine or my officer's application for the purpose.

Enclosed is the latitudes and longitudes of several islands, &c. we discovered during our voyage, the state of the *Pandora*'s company, a list of pirates belonging to the *Bounty*, taken at Otaheite and a list of convicts, deserters from the colony at Port Jackson. It may be necessary to observe that these last have several names, and that William Bryant and James Cox pretend that their time of transportation has expired, but these two then found a boat and money to procure necessaries to enable themselves and others to escape, for which I presume they are liable to punishment, and think it my duty to give information.

Although I have not had the good fortune to fully accomplish the object of my voyage, and that it has in other respects been strongly marked with great misfortunes, I hope it will be thought that the first is not for want of perseverance, or the latter for want of the care and attention of myself and those under my command, but that the disappointment and misfortune arose from the difficulties and peculiar circumstances of the service we were upon; that those of my orders I have been able to fulfil, with the discoveries that have been made will be some compensation for the disappointment and misfortunes that have attended us, and should their Lordships upon the whole think that the voyage will be profitable to our country it will be a great consolation to,

Sir, Your most humble and obedient servant,

Edward Edwards

Philip Stevens Esq.

CAPE OF GOOD HOPE
19TH MARCH, 1792

Sir, Agreeable to my intentions which I did myself the honour to signify to you in a letter addressed from Batavia and sent by a Dutch packet bound to Europe, I embarked the remainder of the company of His Majesty's ship *Pandora*, pirates late belonging to the *Bounty* and the convicts deserters from Port Jackson, on board three Dutch East India ships as follows:—

Myself, the master, Purser, Gunner, Clerk, two midshipmen, twenty-one seamen, and ten pirates on board the *Vreedenburg*, bound to Amsterdam.

Lieutenant Corner, the surgeon, three midshipmen, fourteen seamen, and half the convicts on board the *Horssen*, bound to Rotterdam, and Lieutenant Hayward, the boatswain, surgeon's mate, three midshipmen, fifteen seamen and the other half of the convicts on board the *Hoornwey*, bound to Rotterdam.

Lieutenant Larkin with two petty officers and eighteen seamen were embarked on board the *Zwan* and sailed from Batavia previous to the date of my former letter, and I am now informed that she has been at this port and sailed from hence for Europe more than a month before my arrival. I found His Majesty's Ship *Gorgon* here on her return from Port Jackson, and on account both of expedition and greater security I intend to avail myself of the opportunity to embark on board of her with the ten pirates for England, and I request that you will be pleased to communicate the circumstances to My Lords Commissioners of the Admiralty.

I have the honour to be, Sir,

Your most obedient and humble servant,

Edward Edwards

ADMIRALTY OFFICE

JUNE, 19TH 1792

Sir, I beg leave to inform you that I found His Majesty's Ship *Gorgon* at the Cape of Good Hope on my arrival there in the *Vreedenburg*, a Dutch East India Company's ship, from Batavia, and I thought it proper to remove the pirates late belonging to His Majesty's armed vessel, the *Bounty*, and the convicts, deserters from Port Jackson (whom I had under my charge on board the Dutch East India Company's ships) into His Majesty's said ship, for their greater security, and I took the same opportunity myself to embark on board on her for England and I hope that these steps will be approved of by their Lordships.

I gave you an account of my arrival at the Cape of Good Hope and of my intentions to embark on board the *Gorgon* with the pirates, convicts, &c. in a letter which I did myself the honour to address to you from thence and sent by the *Baring*, Thomas Fingey, Master, an American ship bound to Ostend.

Enclosed is the state of the company of His Majesty's Ship *Pandora* at the time I left the Cape of Good Hope, and the manner in which they were disposed of on board Dutch East India Company's ships in order to be brought to Europe and also a list of the pirates late belonging to the *Bounty*, and of the convicts, deserters from Port Jackson, delivered to me by Mr. Wanjon, the Governor of the Dutch settlements in the island of Timor, now on board His Majesty's Ship *Gorgon*.

I arrived yesterday evening at St. Helens, left the *Gorgon*, and landed at Portsmouth last night and I am now at this office awaiting their Lordships' Commands.

And I have the honour to be, Sir,

Your most obedient and humble servant,

Edward Edwards

Philip Stevens, Esq.

A list of convicts, deserters from Port Jackson, delivered to Captain Edward Edwards of His Majesty's Ship *Pandora* by Timotheus Wanjon, Governor of the Dutch Settlements at Timor, 5th October, 1791.

William Allen	On board H.M.S. *Gorgon*
John Butcher	On board H.M.S. *Gorgon*
Nathaniel Lilley	On board H.M.S. *Gorgon*
James Martin	On board H.M.S. *Gorgon*
Mary Bryant	On board H.M.S. *Gorgon*
William Morton	Died on Dutch East India Co.'s ship, *Hoornwey*
William Bryant	Died 22nd December 1791, Hospital Batavia
James Cox	Deceased, fell overboard Straits of Sunda
John Simms	Died on Dutch East India Co.'s ship *Hoornwey*
Children of the above William and Mary Bryant	
Emanuel Bryant	Died 1st December 1791, Batavia
Charlotte Bryant	Died 6th May 1792 on board H.M.S. *Gorgon*

(Signed) *Edward Edwards*

A list of one petty officer and four seamen lost in a cutter belonging to His Majesty's Ship *Pandora*, at Palmerston's Island on the 24th May, 1791

John Sival	Midshipman
James Good	Seaman
William Wasdel	Seaman
James Scott	Seaman
Joseph Cunningham	Seaman

(Signed) Edward Edwards

LIST OF PIRATES LATE BELONGING TO HIS MAJESTY'S SHIP
BOUNTY TAKEN BY HIS MAJESTY'S SHIP *PANDORA*,
CAPTAIN EDWARD EDWARDS, AT OTAHEITE.

Joseph Coleman	On Board H.M.S. *Gorgon*
Peter Haywood	On Board H.M.S. *Gorgon*
Michael Burn	On Board H.M.S. *Gorgon*
James Morrison	On Board H.M.S. *Gorgon*
Charles Norman	On Board H.M.S. *Gorgon*
Thomas Ellison	On Board H.M.S. *Gorgon*
Thomas MacIntosh	On Board H.M.S. *Gorgon*
William Muspratt	On Board H.M.S. *Gorgon*
Thomas Burkitt	On Board H.M.S. *Gorgon*
John Millward	On Board H.M.S. *Gorgon*
George Stewart	29th August 1791, lost with ship
Richard Skinner	29th August 1791, lost with ship
Henry Heilbrant	29th August 1791, lost with ship
John Sumner	29th August 1791, lost with ship

(Signed) *Edward Edwards*

8, CRAVEN STREET, STRAND
9TH JULY, 1792

Sir, I beg leave to acquaint you that I have information that
the *Vreedenburg* and the *Horssen*, two Dutch East India Company's ships, on board of which part of the company of His Majesty's ship *Pandora* are embarked, were off the Start on the 5th
of this month, on their way to Holland, and that the *Hoornwey*,
the ship on board which the remainder of the company of the
Pandora were embarked, was expected to sail from the Cape of
Good Hope in about three weeks after the two former ships left
that place, but the account does not mention the day they left
the Cape themselves.

I have the honour to be, Sir,
Your most obedient and humble servant,
Edward Edwards

STATE of the Company of H.M.S. *Pandora*, Captain Edward Edwards: and the manner disposed of on board Dutch East India Company's Ships for their voyage to Europe.

	Com. Off. & Master.	Warrant Officers.	Petty Officers.	Seamen.
Zwan, Lt. John Larkan,	1		2	17
Horssen, Lt. Robert Corner,	1	1	2	13
Mr. George Hamilton Surgeon.				
Hornwey, Lt. Thos. Hayward,				
John Cunningham, Boatswain,	1	1	2	14
Vreedenberg, Mr. G. Passmore, Master,				
Mr. Gregory Bentham, Purser,				
Mr. Jos.	1	2	1	18
Parker gunner and 1 Super-numary belonging to H.M. armed vessel *Supply*.				
Hospital at Batavia,				1
H.M.S. *Gorgon*, Captain Edwards,	1		2	1
	5	4	9	64

Whole Number borne,	82
Died since ship was lost,	16
Discharged,	1
Whole number Ship's company saved in ship and tender	99
Supernumaries.	
Do. Pirates,	10
Convicts, 4 men and 1 woman	5

EDWARD EDWARDS.

Names of Islands.	Lat. S.	Long. W.
Mitre Island,	11° 49' 00"	190° 04' 30"
Cherry Island,	11° 37' 30"	190° 19' 30"
Pitt's Isle (South Point),	11° 50' 30"	193° 14' 05"
Wells Shoal on reef,	12° 20' 00"	202° 02' 00"
Cape Rodney,	10° 03' 32"	212° 14' 05"
Mount Clarence between the two Orayas.		
Cape Hood,	9° 58' 06"	212° 37' 10"
Look Out Shoal.		
Stoney Reef Islands.		
Murray's Islands,	9° 57' 00"	216° 43' 00"
Wreck Reef.		
Escape Key,	11° 23' 00"	
Entrance Key,	11° 23' 00"	

EDWARD EDWARDS.

A LIST OF 14 PIRATES, BELONGING TO H.M.S. LATE SHIP *BOUNTY*,
TAKEN AT OTAHEITE.

Joseph Coleman	Peter Haywood
Michael Byrne	James Morrison
Charles Norman	Thomas Ellison
Thomas M'Intosh	William Muspratt
Thomas Burkitt	John Millward
George Stewart	Drowned August 29th 1791
Richard Skinner	Drowned August 29th 1791
Henry Hillbrant	Drowned August 29th 1791
John Sumner	Drowned August 29th 1791

(Signed) *Edward Edwards*

A Voyage Round the World

by George Hamilton
Surgeon of the *Pandora*

Chapter 1

To Punish the Mutineers

Government having resolved to bring to punishment the mutineers of His Majesty's late ship *Bounty*, and to survey the Straits of Endeavour, to facilitate a passage to Botany Bay, on the 10th of August 1790, appointed Captain Edward Edwards to put in commission at Chatham, and take command of the *Pandora* Frigate of twenty-four guns, and a hundred and sixty men.

A great naval armament then equipping retarded our progress, and prevented that particular attention to the choice of men which their Lordships so much wished; as contagion here crept amongst us from infected clothing, the fatal effects of which we discovered, and severely experienced, in the commencement of the voyage.

Every thing necessary being completed, and an additional complement of naval stores, received for the refitment of the *Bounty*; dropped down to Sheerness, saluted Admiral Dalrymple, paid the same compliments to Sir Richard King, in passing the Downs, arrived at Portsmouth, and found there Lord Howe with the Union Flag at the main, and the proudest navy that ever graced the British seas under his command.

Here the officers and men received six months pay in advance, and after receiving their final orders, got the time-keeper on board, weighed anchor, and proceeded to sea.

As the white cliffs of Albion receded from our view alternate hopes and fears took possession of our minds, wafting the last kind *adieu* to our native soil.

We pursued our voyage with a favourable breeze; but *Pandora* now seemed inclined to shed her baneful influence among us, and a malignant fever threatened much havoc, as in a few days thirty-five men were confined to their beds, and unfortunately Mr. Innes, the Surgeon's only mate, was among the first taken ill; what rendered our situation still more distressing, was the crowded state of the ship being filled to the hatchways with stores and provisions, for, like weevils, we had to eat a hole in our bread, before we had a place to lay down in; every officer's cabin, the captain's not excepted, being filled with provisions and stores. Our sufferings were much increased, for want of room to accommodate our sick, notwithstanding every effort of the captain that humanity could suggest.

In this sickly lumbered state, near the latitude of Madeira, we observed a sail bearing down upon us: from her appearance and manoeuvres, we had every reason to believe she was a ship of war; and a rumour of a Spanish war prevailing when we left England, rendered it necessary to clear ship for action; as soon as our guns were run out, and all hands at quarters, got along side of her, when she proved His Majesty's Ship, *Shark*, sent out with orders of recall to Admiral Cornish, who had sailed for the West Indies a few days before we left Spithead.

This little disaster deranged us much, having at the same time bad weather, attended with heavy thunder squalls. The Peek of Tenerife now began to show his venerable crest, towering above the clouds; and in two days more came to an anchor in the road of Santa Cruz, but did not salute, as the commandant had not authority to return it.

Immediately on our arrival we were boarded by the Portmaster, by whom we learnt they had been in much apprehension of a disagreeable visit from the English, but were happy to hear that matters were amicably settled between the Courts of Madrid and St. James's.

With respect to site nothing can be more beautifully picturesque than the town of Santa Cruz. It stands in the centre of a spacious bay, on a gentle acclivity surrounded with retiring hills, and the noble promontory of the Peek rising majestically behind it, dignifies the scene beyond description, being continually diversified with every vicissitude of the surrounding atmosphere, emerging and retiring thro' the fleecy clouds, from the bottom of the mountain to its summit.

All the circumjacent hills on the margin of the beach are tufted with little forts, and *barbette* batteries, forming an Esplanade round the bay, affords a most agreeable landscape. The houses being all painted white, pretty regularly built, and standing on a rising ground, raises one street above another, and heightens the scene from the water; to which the Governor's garden contributes much to beautify the town.

In the centre of the principal square, is a well built fountain, continually playing, which, in a warm climate, has a desirable cooling effect. There is but one church, which contains a few indifferent paintings.

The inhabitants are civil, but reserved, and the inquisition being on the island, spreads a gloomy distrust on the countenance of the people.

The troops are miserably clothed, and poverty and superstition lord it wide. The wines of this place, from a late improvement in the vines, are equal to the second kind of Madeira, and I cannot pass over this subject without making honourable mention of the candour of Mr. Rooney our wine merchant.

Here we completed our water from an aqueduct admirably constructed for the convenience of the shipping, and after receiving on board lemons, oranges, pomegranates, and bananas, with every variety of fruits and other refreshments with which this island most plentifully abounds, proceeded again on our voyage.

The fever that prevailed on our leaving England became now pretty general, and almost every man had it in turn, and as we approached the line many of the convalescents had a relapse, but the Lords of the Admiralty, previous to our sailing, had supplied us with such unbounded liberality in every thing necessary for the preservation of the seamens' health, that I may venture to say many lives were saved from their bounty, and I should be wanting in my duty to their Lordships, as well as the community, was I to pass over in silence the uncommon good effects we experienced from supplying the sick and convalescent with tea and sugar; this being the first time it has ever been introduced into his Majesty's service; but it is an article in life that has crept into such universal use, in all orders of society, that it needs no comment of mine to recommend it. It may, however, be easily conceived that it will be sought with more avidity by those whose aliment consists chiefly in animal food, and that always salt, and often of the worst kind. Their bread too is generally mixed with oatmeal, and of a hot drying nature. Scarcity of water is a calamity to which seafaring people are always subject; and it is an established fact, that a pint of tea will satiate thirst more than a quart of water. But when sickness takes place, a loathing of all animal food follows; then tea becomes their sole existence, and that which can be conveyed to them as natural food will be taken with pleasure, when any slip slop, given as drink, will be rejected with disgust. Suffice it to say, that Quarter-masters, and real good seamen have ever been observed to be regular in cooking their little pot of tea or coffee, and in America seamen going long voyages, always make it an article in their agreement to be supplied with tea and sugar.

The air now becoming intolerably hot, and to evacuate the foul air from below where the people slept, had recourse to Mr. White's new ventilator, but found little benefit from it; not from any fault in the machine, but from the crowded state of the ship, it was impossible to throw a current of air into those places where it was most wanted, but by the addition of a flexible leather tube, like a water engine, it might be rendered of the utmost importance to the service, as in tenders' press-holds, and in line-of-battle ships at sea, when the lower deck ports cannot be opened; where often the jail fever, and all the calamities that attend human nature in crowded situations, are engendered, that might be entirely obviated by Mr. White's ingenious machine. I should beg to recommend wheels to be substituted for legs to it, for its easier conveyance from one part of the ship to the other, and that he would sacrifice beauty to strength, as a slight mahogany jim crack is not well calculated to the severity of heat we are exposed to, in climates where it is most wanted.

There were now many water spouts about the ship, at which

we fired several guns: the thermometer fluctuated between seventy-nine and eighty, and without any thing worthy of remark, in the common occurrence of things at sea, on the twenty-eight of December saw the land of the Brazils, and in two days saluted the fort at Rio de Janiero with fifteen guns, which was immediately returned.

On our coming to anchor, an officer came to acquaint the captain, that a party of soldiers should be sent on board of us, agreeable to their custom, which was most peremptorily denied as inadmissible with the dignity of the British flag, nor would Captain Edwards go on shore to pay his respects to the Vice Roy, till that etiquette was settled, that his boat should not be boarded.

After the usual compliments were paid the Vice Roy, his suit of carriages were ordered to attend the British officers, and Monsieur le Font, the Surgeon-General, who spoke English with ease and fluency, showed us every mark of politeness and attention on the occasion, in carrying us through the principal streets, then visited the public gardens, built by the late Vice Roy, and laid out with much taste and expense. All the extremity of the garden is a fine terrace which commands a view of the water, and is frequented by people of fashion, as their Grand Mall: at each end of the terrace there is an octagonal built room, superbly furnished, where merendas[1] are sometimes given. On the panels are painted the various productions and commerce of South America, representing the diamond fishery, the process of the indigo trade. The rice grounds and harvest, sugar plantation, South Sea whale fishery, &c. these were interspersed with views of the country, and the quadrupeds that inhabit those parts. The ceilings contained all the variety, the one of the fish, the other of the fowl of that continent. The compartments of the ceiling of the one room was enriched in shell work, with all the variegated shells of that country, and in the compartments are delineated all the variety of fish that the coast of South America produces. The other compartment is enriched with feathers and so inimitably blended as to produce the happiest effect. In this ceiling is painted all the birds and fowls of the country, in all

1. Afternoon entertainments.

their splendid elegance of plumage. The sofas and furniture are rich in the extreme: and in this elegant recess, an idle traveller may have an agreeable lounge, and at one view comprehend the whole natural history of this vast continent. In the centre of the terrace there is a *jet d'eau*, in form of a large palm-tree, made of copper, which at pleasure may be made to spout water from the extremity of all the leaves. This tree stands on a well disposed grotto, which rises from the gravel walk below to the level of the terrace, and terminates the view of the principal walk. Near the foot of the grotto two large alligators, made of copper, are continually discharging water into a handsome basin of white marble, filled with gold and silver fishes.

There are fine orangeries, and lofty covered arbours in different parts of the garden, capable of containing a thousand people. Here the Cyprian nymphs hold their nocturnal revels; but intrigue is attended with great danger, as the stiletto is in general use, and assassination frequent, the men being of a jealous sanguinary turn, and the women fond of gallantry, who never appear in public unveiled. When Bougainville, the French circumnavigator called here, his chaplain was assassinated in an affray of that kind; but since that accident, orders were given that a commissioned officer should attend all foreign officers, and a soldier the privates; and all strangers, on landing, are conducted to the main guard for their escort. This answers a double purpose, as they are much afraid of strangers smuggling or carrying money out of the country, under the mask of personal protection, every motion is watched and scrutinized, nor can you purchase any thing of a merchant, till he has settled with the officer of the police how much he shall exact for his goods; so you have always the satisfaction of being robbed as the act directs.

The trade of this country is much cramped by the improper policy of the mother country; for although it abounds with every thing that the earth produces, wealth is far from being diffusive, and a spirit for revolt seems to prevail amongst them; but they were rather premature in business, a conspiracy being detected whilst we were there, many of the first people in the country thrown into dungeons, a strong guard put over them, and all intercourse denied them. But in order to check that spirit of rebellion among the colonists, a regiment of black slaves is now embodied, who will be very ready to bear arms against their oppressive masters; but should a revolution in South America take place, which sooner or later must eventually happen, some of our South Sea discoveries would then prove an advantageous situation for a little British colony.

All public works are done here by slaves in chains, who perform a kind of plaintive melancholy dirge in recitative, to sooth their unavailing toil, which, with the accompaniment of the clanking of their irons, is the real voice of woe, and attunes the soul to sympathy and compassion, more than the most elaborate piece of music.

The troops are remarkably well clothed, and in fine order, both infantry and cavalry; the horses are small, but spirited, and tournaments frequently performed as the favourite amusement of the inhabitants, at which the cavaliers display a wonderful share of address.

The town is large, built of stone, and the streets very regular; there are several handsome churches, monasteries, and nunneries, and contains about forty thousand inhabitants; but, like the old town of Edinburgh, each floor contains a distinct family, and of course liable to the same inconveniencies, cleanliness being none of its most shining virtues.

The officers of the army showed us uncommon kindness, and made us some presents of red bird skins for the savages we were going amongst.

I cannot, in words, bestow sufficient panegyric on the laudable exertions of my worthy messmates, Lieutenants Corner and Hayward, for their unremitting zeal in procuring and nursing such plants as might be useful at Otaheitee or the islands we might discover.

We now took leave of our friends here, and it was with some regret, as it was bidding adieu to civilized life, for a very undetermined space of time. Lieutenant Hayward having finished his astronomical observations on shore, came on board with the time-keeper and instruments, and again proceeded on our voyage, on the morning of January 8, 1791. In running down the coast of the Brazils, saw several spermaceti whales, and vessels employed on that fishery. Could it have been accomplished in the month of January, it was intended to take in a supply of water at New-Year's harbour, but the season was too far advanced. The weather now became cold, and the health of the people mended apace: passed by the straits of Magellan, and on the 31st of January saw Cape St. Juan, Staten Island, and New-Year's Island. The thermometer was at 48 degrees. We were fortunate enough to weather the tempestuous regions of Cape Horn, without any thing remarkable happening, although late in the season.

The weather, as we advanced, became now exceedingly pleasant, and the many good things with which we were supplied, began to have a wonderful good effect on the strength of our convalescents. I here beg the reader's indulgence for a small digression on the health of the seamen, as it is a subject of much national importance, and those voyages the only test of what is found to succeed best, my duty leads me to the attempt, however unequal to the task:

It may be remarked, the sauerkraut kept during the voyage, in the highest perfection, and was often eat as a salad with vinegar, in preference to recent, cut vegetables from the shore. A cask of this grand antiscorbutic was kept open for the crew to eat as much of as they pleased; and I will venture to affirm, that it will answer every purpose that can be expected from the vegetable kingdom.

The Essence of Malt afforded a most delightful beverage, and, with the addition of a little hops, in the warmest climates, made as good strong beer as we could in England. We were likewise supplied with malt in grain, but should prefer the essence, as it is less liable to decay, and stows in much less room, which is a very valuable consideration in long voyages.

Cocoa we found great benefit from; it is much relished by the men, stows in little room, and affords great nourishment. At the close of the war in 1783, in the West Indies, men that had been the whole war on salt provisions, from a liberal use of the cocoa, got fat and strong, and in the *Agamemnon* we had five hundred men who had served most of the war on salt provisions; but after the cocoa was introduced, we had not a sick man on board till the day she was paid off. Indeed it is the only article of nourishment in sea victualling; for what can in reason be expected from beef or pork after it has been salted a year or two?

Wheat we found answer extremely well, rough ground in a mill occasionally as we wanted it, and with the addition of a little brown sugar, it made a pleasant nourishing diet, of which the men were extremely fond. Another great advantage attending it, that it does not require half the quantity of water that peas do.

Soft bread was found extremely beneficial to the sick and convalescent, and we availed ourselves of every opportunity of baking for half the complement at a time. As the flour keeps so much longer sound than biscuit, it may be needless to remark its superior advantages; besides, it is not liable to be damaged by water or otherwise, so much as bread, as a crust forms outside, which protects the rest. In point of stowage it likewise is preferable.

As the fate of every expedition of this kind depends much on the exertion of the subordinate departments of office, the thanks of every individual in the *Pandora* is due to Mr. Cherry, for his uncommon attention to the victualling.

The dividing the people into three watches had a double good effect as it gave them longer time to sleep, and dry themselves before they turned in; and as most of our crew consisted of landsmen, the fewer people being on deck at a time, rendered it necessary to exert themselves more in learning their duty.

The air became now temperate, mild, and agreeable; but unfortunately we sprung a leak in the after part of the ship, which reached the bread room, and damaged much of it, as one thousand five hundred and fifteen pounds were thrown over-board, and a great deal much injured, that we kept for feeding the cattle. Many blue Petrels were seen flying about, and on the 4th of March saw Easter Island. We now set the forge to work, and the armourers were busily employed in making knives and iron work to trade with the savages. On the 16th we discovered a Lagoon Island of about three or four miles extent; it was well wooded, but had no inhabitants, and was named Ducie's Island, in honour of Lord Ducie.

On the 17th we discovered another Island, about five or six miles long, with a great many trees on it, but was not inhabited: this was called Lord Hood's Island.

On the 19th we discovered an Island of the same description as the former, which was named Carrisfort Island, in honour of Lord Carrisfort.

On the 22nd passed Maitea, and on the morning of the 23rd of March anchored in Matavy bay, in the Island of Otaheitee. In the dawn of the morning, a native immediately on seeing us, paddled off in his canoe, and came on board, who showed expressions of joy to a degree of madness, on embracing and saluting us, by whom we learnt that several of the mutineers were on the island; but that Mr. Christian and nine men had left Otaheitee long since in the *Bounty*, and amused the natives, by telling them Captain Bligh had gone to settle at Whytutakee, and that Captain Cook was living there. Language cannot express his surprise on Lieutenant Hayward's being introduced to him, who had been purposely concealed.

At eleven in the forenoon the launch and pinnace was dispatched with Lieutenants Corner and Hayward and twenty-six men, to the north west part of the island, in quest of mutineers. Immediately on our arrival, Joseph Coleman, the armourer of the *Bounty*, came on board, and a little after the two midshipmen belonging to the *Bounty*; at three Richard Skinner came off, and on the 25th the boats returned, after chasing the mutineers on shore, and taking possession of their boat. As they had taken to the heights, and claimed the protection of Tamarrah, a great chief in Papara, who was the proper king of Otaheitee, the present family of Ottoo being usurpers, and who intended, had we not arrived with the assistance of the *Bounty*'s people, to have disputed the point with Ottoo.

On the twenty-seventh we sent the Pinnace with a present of a bottle of rum to king Ottoo, who was with his two queens at Tiaraboo, requesting the honour of his company, but the bottle of rum removed all scruples, and next day the royal family paid us a visit, and in his suit came Oedidy, a chief particularly noticed by Captain Cook.

On the first visit they make it a point of honour of accepting of no present; but they make sufficient amends for that, by introducing a numerous train of dependents afterwards, to obtain presents.

The King is a tall handsome looking man, about six feet three inches high, good natured, and affable in his manners. His principal queen, Edea, is a robust looking, course woman, about thirty, and was extremely solicitous in learning and adopting our customs, and on hearing our English ladies drank tea, became very fond of it. The other queen, or concubine, named Aeredy, is a pretty young creature, about sixteen years of age: they all three sleep together, and live in the most perfect harmony.

A detachment of men were immediately ordered, under the command of Lieutenant Corner, to march across the country, and if possible to get between the mountains and the mutineers; this gentleman was extremely well calculated for an expedition of this kind, having, in the early part of his life, bore a commission in the land service, and next morning they landed on Point Venus, attended by the principal chiefs as conductors, and a number of the common people to assist in carrying the ammunition over the heights: what rendered their assistance more necessary, was their having to cross a rapid cataract, or river, which came down from the mountains, and formed so many curves. They had to ford it sixteen times in the course of their journey, which gave evident proofs of the superior strength of the natives over the English seamen. The former went over with ease, where the sailors could not stem the rapidity of the torrent without their help. They were, however, forced to send to the ship for ropes and tackles to gain some heights which were otherwise inaccessible.

On the party coming to a rest, the lieutenant expressed a wish to one of the natives for something to eat, who told him he might be supplied with plenty of victuals ready dressed; he immediately ran to a temple, or place of worship, where meat was regularly served to their god, and came running with a roasted pig, that had been presented that day. This striking instance of impiety rather startled the lieutenant, which the other easily got over, by saying there was more left than the god could eat.

It was with much difficulty they could restrain the natives from committing depredations on the Cava grounds of the upper districts, as they were on the eve of a war with them respecting the hereditary right of the crown.

The party now arrived at the residence of a great chief, who received them with much hospitality and kindness; and after refreshing them with plenty of meat and drink, carried the officer to visit the Morai of the dead chief, his father. Mr. Corner judging it necessary, by every mark of attention, to gain the good graces of this great man, ordered his party to draw up, and fire three volleys over the deceased, who was brought out in his best new clothes, on the occasion; but the burning cartridge from one of the muskets, unfortunately set fire to the paper clothes of the dead chief. This unlucky disaster threw the son into the greatest perplexity, as agreeable to their laws, should the corpse of his father be stolen away, or otherwise destroyed, he forfeits his title and estate, and it descends to the next heir.

There was at the same time a party embarked by water, under the command of Lieutenant Hayward, who took with him some of the principal chiefs, amongst whom was Oedidy, before mentioned by Captain Cook, who went a voyage with him, but fell into disrepute amongst them, from affirming he had seen water in a solid form; alluding to the ice. He also took with him one Brown, an Englishman, that had been left on shore by an American vessel that had called there, for being troublesome on board: but otherwise a keen, penetrating, active fellow, who rendered many eminent services, both in this expedition and the subsequent part of the voyage. He had lived upwards of twelve months amongst the natives, adopted perfectly their manners and customs, even to the eating of raw fish, and dipping his roast pork into a cocoa nut shell of salt water, according to their manner, as substitute for salt. He likewise avoided all intercourse and communication with the *Bounty*'s people, by which means necessity forced him to gain a pretty competent knowledge of their language; and from natural complexion was much darker than any of the natives.

Captain Edwards had taken every possible means of gaining

the friendship of Tamarrah, the great prince of the upper district, by sending him very liberal presents, which effectually brought him over to our interest. The mutineers were now cut off from every hope of resource; the natives were harassing them behind, and Mr. Hayward and his party advancing in front; under cover of night they had taken shelter in a hut in the woods, but were discovered by Brown, who creeping up to the place where they were asleep, distinguished them from the natives by feeling their toes; as people unaccustomed to wear shoes are easily discovered from the spread of their toes. Next day Mr. Hayward attacked them, but they grounded their arms without opposition; their hands were bound behind their back and sent down to the boat under a strong guard.

During the whole business there was only two natives killed; one was shot in the dusk of the evening, two nights before the people surrendered, by one of the sentinels, who had his musket twice beat out of his hand from the natives pelting our party with large stones; but the instant he was shot, some of his friends rushed in and carried off the corpse.

The other native was shot by the mutineers; when attacked by the natives they took to a river; a stone being thrown by one of the natives at the wife, or woman, of one of the mutineers, enraged him so much, that he immediately shot the offender.

A prison was built for their accommodation on the quarter deck, that they might be secure, and apart from our ship's company; and that it might have every advantage of a free circulation of air, which rendered it the most desirable place in the ship. Orders were likewise given that they should be victualled, in every respect in the same as the ship's company, both in meat, liquor, and all the extra indulgencies with which we were so liberally supplied, notwithstanding the established laws of the service, which restricts prisoners to two-thirds allowance: but Captain Edwards very humanely commiserated with their unhappy and inevitable length of confinement. Oripai, the king's brother, a discerning, sensible, and intelligent chief, discovered a conspiracy amongst the natives on shore to cut our cables should it come to blow hard from the sea. This was more to be dreaded, as many of the prisoners were married to the most respectable chiefs' daughters in the district opposite to where we lay at anchor; in particular one, who took the name of Stewart, a man of great possession in landed property, near Matavy Bay: a gentleman of that name belonging to the *Bounty* having married his daughter, and he, as his friend and father-in law, agreeable to their custom, took his name.

Ottoo the king, his two brothers, and all the principal chiefs, appeared extremely anxious for our safety; and after the prisoners were on board, kept watch during the night; were always keeping a sharp look out upon our cables, and continually spurring the sentinels to be careful in their duty. The prisoners' wives visited the ship daily and brought their children, who were permitted to be carried to their unhappy fathers. To see the poor captives in irons, weeping over their tender offspring, was too moving a scene for any feeling heart. Their wives brought them ample supplies of every delicacy that the country afforded while we lay there, and behaved with the greatest fidelity and affection to them.

Next day the king, his two queens, and retinue, came on board to pay us a formal visit, preceded by a band of music. The ladies had about sixty or seventy yards of Otaheitee cloth wrapt round them, and were so bulky and unwieldy with it, they were obliged to be hoisted on board like horn cattle: hogs, cocoanuts, bananas, a rich sort of peach, and a variety of ready dressed puddings and victuals, composed their present to the captain.

As soon as they were on board, the captain *debarassoit* the ladies, by rolling their linen round his middle; an indispensable ceremony here in receiving a present of cloth: and Medua, wife to Oripai, the king's brother, took a great liking to the captain's laced coat, which he immediately put on her with much gallantry; and that beautiful princess seemed much elated with her new finery. I cannot omit a circumstance of this lady's attachment to dress. There was a custom which had prevailed for a long time, to present the god with all red feathers that could be procured; but thinking she would become red feathers full as well as his godship, immediately employed all her domestics making them up into fly flaps, and other personal ornaments, to prevent the altar making a monopoly of all the good things, in this, as well as in other countries.

A grand Haeva was next day ordered for our entertainment ashore, on Point Venus, and on our landing we were preceded by a band of music, and led to where the king and his levee were in waiting to receive us. The course was soon cleared by the chiefs, and the entertainment began by two men, who vied with each other in filthy lascivious attitudes, and frightful distortions of their mouths. These having performed their part, two ladies, pretty fancifully dressed, as described in Captain Cook's Voyages, were introduced after a little ceremony. Something resembling a turkey-cock's tail, and stuck on their rumps in a fan kind of fashion, about five feet in diameter, had a very good effect while the ladies kept their faces to us; but when in a bending attitude, they presented their rumps, to show the wonderful agility of their loins; the effect is better conceived than described. After half an hour's hard exercise, the dear creatures had *remüé* themselves into a perfect furore, and the piece concluded by the ladies exposing that which is better felt than seen; and, in that state of nature, walked from the bottom of the theatre to the top where we were sitting on the grass, till they approached just by us, and then we complimented them in bowing, with all the honours of war.

These accomplishments are so much prized amongst them that girls come from the interior parts of the country to the court residence, for improvement in the Haeva, just as country gentlemen send their daughters to London boarding-schools.

This may well be called the Cythera of the southern hemisphere, not only from the beauty and elegance of the women, but their being so deeply versed in, and so passionately fond of the Eleusinian mysteries; and what poetic fiction has painted of Eden, or Arcadia, is here realized, where the earth without tillage produces both food and clothing, the trees loaded with the richest of fruit, the carpet of nature spread with the most odoriferous flowers, and the fair ones ever willing to fill your arms with love.

It affords a happy instance of contradicting an opinion propagated by philosophers of a less bountiful soil, who maintain that every virtuous or charitable act a man commits, is from selfish and interested views. Here human nature appears in more amiable colours, and the soul of man, free from the gripping hand of want, acts with a liberality and bounty that does honour to his God.

A native of this country divides every thing in common with his friend, and the extent of the word friend, by them, is only bounded by the universe, and was he reduced to his last morsel of bread, he cheerfully halves it with him; the next that comes has the same claim, if he wants it, and so in succession to the last mouthful he has. Rank makes no distinction in hospitality; for the king and beggar relieve each other in common.

The English are allowed by the rest of the world, and I believe with some degree of justice, to be a generous, charitable people; but the Otaheiteans could not help bestowing the most contemptuous word in their language upon us, which is, *peery peery*, or stingy.

In becoming the *tyo*, or friend of a man, it is expected you pay him a compliment, by cherishing his wife; but, being ignorant of that ceremony, I very innocently gave high offence to Matuara, the king of York Island, to whom I was introduced as his friend: a shyness took place on the side of his Majesty, from my neglect to his wife; but, through the medium of Brown the interpreter, he put me in mind of my duty, and on my promising my endeavours, matters were for that time made up. It was to me, however, a very serious inauguration: I was, in the first place, not a young man, and had been on shore a whole week; the lady was a woman of rank, being sister to Ottoo, the king of Otaheite, and had in her youth been beautiful, and named Peggy Ottoo. She is the right hand dancing figure so elegantly delineated in Cook's Voyages. But Peggy had seen much service, and bore away many honourable scars in the fields of Venus. However, his Majesty's service must be done, and Matuara and I were again friends. He was a domesticated man, and passionately fond of his wife and children; but now became pensive and melancholy, dreading the child should be Piebald; though the lady was six months advanced in her pregnancy before we came to the island.

The force of friendship amongst those good creatures, will be more fully understood from the following circumstance: Churchill, the principal ringleader of the mutineers, on his landing, became the *tyo*, or friend, of a great chief in the upper districts. Some time after the chief happening to die without issue, his title and estate, agreeable to their law from *tyoship*, devolved on Churchill, who having some dispute with one Thomson of the *Bounty*, was shot by him. The natives immediately rose, and revenged the death of Churchill their chief, by killing Thomson, whose skull was afterwards shown to us, which bore evident marks of fracture.

Oedidy, although perfectly devoted to our interest, on being appointed one of the guides in the expedition against the mutineers, expressed great horror at the act he was going to commit, in betraying his friend, being Tyo to one of them.

They are much less addicted to thieving than when Captain Cook visited them; and when things were stolen, by applying to the magistrate of the district, the goods were immediately returned; for, like every other well regulated police, the thief and justice were of one gang.

Sometimes we slightly punished the offenders, by cutting off their hair. A beautiful young creature, who lived at the Observatory with one of our young gentlemen, slipped out of bed from him in the night, and stole all his linen. She was punished for the theft, by shaving one of her eye-brows, and half of the hair off her head. She immediately run into the woods, and used to come once or twice a day to the tent, to request looking at herself in the glass; but the grotesque figure she cut, with one side entirely bald, made her shriek out, and run into the woods to shun society.

With respect to agriculture, in a soil where nature has done so much, little is left to human industry; but had there been occasion for it, abilities would not be wanting. It is much to be lamented, that the endeavours of the philanthropic Sir Joseph

Banks were frustrated, by their razing of every thing which he took so much pains to rear amongst them, a few shaddocks excepted. Tobacco and cotton have escaped their ravage; and they are much mortified that they cannot eradicate it from their grounds: but were a handloom on a simple construction, as used by the natives of Java, introduced amongst them, they could soon turn their cotton to good account. An instance of their ingenuity and imitative powers in matting, was a thing perfectly unknown amongst them till Captain Cook introduced it from Anamooka, one of the Friendly Isles: but in that branch of manufacture they now far surpass their original. They have likewise abundance of fine sugarcanes, growing spontaneously all over the island, from which rum and sugar might be extracted. Indeed an attempt was made by Coleman, the armourer of the *Bounty*, who made a still, and succeeded; but, dreading the effects of intoxication, both amongst themselves and the natives, very wisely put an end to his labours by breaking the still.

Captain Bligh has likewise planted Indian corn, from which much may be expected. On our landing, as soon as public business of more importance would permit, our gentlemen were indefatigable in laying out a piece of garden ground, and ditching it round. Lemons, oranges, limes, pine-apples, plants of the coffee tree, with all the lesser class of things, as onions, lettuces, peas, cabbages, and every thing necessary for culinary purposes, were planted.

In order that they might not meet the same fate of the things planted by Sir Joseph Banks, Captain Edwards made use of every stratagem to make the chiefs fond of the oranges and limes, by dipping them in sugar, to cover the acid before it be presented to them to eat. Messrs. Corner and Hayward were equally zealous in using the most persuasive arguments with the chiefs to take care of our garden, and rear and propagate the plants when we were gone; to all which they lent a deaf ear, and treated the subject with much levity, saying, they might be very good to us, but that they were already plentifully supplied with every thing they wished or wanted, and had not occasion for more. But on the lieutenant's representing, that if, on our return, they could supply us with plenty of such articles as we left with them, they in exchange would receive hatchets, knives, and red cloth, they seemed more favourably inclined to our project; and I have no doubt but that some after navigators will reap the benefit of their industry.

The Bread-fruit, although the most delicate and nourishing food upon earth, is, with people like them, liable to inconveniencies; for in such a group or Archipelago of islands, whose inhabitants are in such various gradations of refinement, from the gentle and polished Otaheitean, to the savage and cannibal Feegee, a war amongst them is often attended with devastation as well as famine. By cutting round the bark of the Bread-fruit tree, a whole country may be laid waste for four or five years, young trees not bearing in less time. Crops, such as Indian corn, English wheat and peas, that have been left amongst them, can in time of war be stored in granaries on the top of their almost inaccessible mountains.

While speaking of the Breadfruit tree, I can exemplify my subject from what happened to an island contiguous to Otaheite, whose coast abounded with fine fish; and the Otaheitans, being themselves too lazy to catch them, destroyed all the Bread-fruit trees on this little island; by which act of policy, they are obliged to send over boats with fish regularly to market, to be supplied with bread in barter from Otaheite. To this island they likewise send their wives, thinking they become fair by living on fish, and low diet. They also send boys for the same reason, whom they keep for abominable purposes.

As to the religion of this country, it is difficult for me to define it. Their tenets, although equally ignorant of heathen mythology or theological intricacies, seem to partake of both; and, like other nations in the early ages of society, are rendered subservient to political purposes, as by the machinery of deification the person of the king is sacred and inviolable. Notwithstanding the king be a broad shouldered strapping fellow, three sturdy stallions of *cecisbeos*, or lords in waiting, are kept for the particular amusement of the queen, when his majesty is in his cups. Yet the royal issue is always declared to be sprung from the immortal Gods; and the heir-apparent, during his minority, is put under the tuition of the high priest. Their God is supposed to be omnipresent, and is worshipped in spirit, idolatry not being known amongst them. The sacred mysteries are only known to the priests or augurs, the king, princes, and great chiefs, the common people only serving as victims, or to fill up the pageantry of a religious procession. One of our gentlemen expressing a wish to the high priest, of carrying from amongst them that God whose altars craved so much human blood, he, like a true priest, had his subterfuge ready, by saying, there were more of the same family in the other islands, from whence they could easily be supplied. On all great occasions, each district sends a male victim; and the island containing forty districts, it may be presumed the mortality is great. Between the sacrifices and the ravages of war, a preponderating number of females must have taken place; to counteract which, a law passed, that every other female child should be put to death at birth; and the husband always officiating as *acoucheur* to his wife, the child is destroyed as soon as the sex is discovered.

The absurdity of this inhuman law is now pretty evident. Women are become more scarce, and set a higher value on their charms, which occasions many desperate battles amongst them. Some with fractured skulls were sent on board of us, which had been got in amorous affrays of that kind.

It may naturally be supposed, that people of such gentle natures make no conspicuous figure in the theatre of war.

Their war-canoes are very large, on which a platform is placed, capable of containing from a hundred and fifty to two hundred men. But their taste in decorating the prow of their men of war, plainly indicates they are more versed in the fields of Venus than Mars, every man of war having a figure head of the god Priapus, with a preposterous insignia of his order; the sight of which never fails to excite great glee and good humour amongst the ladies.

It is customary with those nations at war, that the treaty of peace be confirmed by the conquerors sending a certain number of their women to cohabit with the nation that is vanquished, in order to conciliate their affection by a bond more lasting than wax and parchment. It was the unhappy lot of Otaheite to be overcome by a nation whose women were too masculine for them; they being accustomed to the amorous dalliance of their own beautiful females, were averse to familiar intercourse with strangers. The ladies returned with all the rage of disappointed women, and the war was renewed with all its horrors.

They are well acquainted with the bow and arrow, but use it as an amusement. The only missive weapons they use are the sling and spear. They have now amongst them about twenty stand of arms, and two hundred rounds of powder and ball. They can take a musket to pieces, and put it up again; are good marksmen, take proper care of their arms and ammunition; and are highly sensible of the superior advantage it gives them over the neighbouring nations.

In the preparing and printing their cloth, the women display a great share of ingenuity and good taste. Many of their figures were exactly the patterns which prevailed, as fashionable, when we left England, both striped and figured. They print their figured cloth by dipping the leaves in dye-stuffs of different colours, placing them as their fancy directs. Their cloth is of different texture of fineness, from a stuff of the same nature in quality as the slightest India paper, to a kind as durable as some of our cottons; but they will not bear water, and of course become troublesome and expensive. They are generally made up in bales, running about two yards broad, and twenty or thirty yards long. We had some thousands of yards of it sent on board as presents.

Their sumptuary laws, at first sight, may appear severe towards the fair sex, who are not permitted to eat butcher-meat, nor to eat at all, in the presence of their husbands. It certainly does not convey the most delicate ideas, to a mind impressed with much sensibility, to see a fine woman devouring a piece of beef; and those voluptuaries, who may be said to exist only by their women, would naturally endeavour to remove the possibility of presupposing a disgusting idea in that object in which all their happiness centres.

Every woman, the queen and royal family excepted, on the

approach of the king, is denuded down to the waist, and continues so whilst his majesty is in sight. Should the king enter a woman's house, it is immediately pulled down. The king is never permitted to help himself with meat or drink, which makes him a very troublesome visitor, as he is never quiet whilst a bottle is in sight till he has had the last drop of it.

Their houses are well adapted to the temperate climate they inhabit, and generally consist of three chambers, the interior one of which the chief retires to, after he has drank his cava. A profound silence is observed during his repose; for should they be suddenly awaked, it produces violent vomiting, and a train of uneasy sensations; but, otherwise, if undisturbed, it proves a safe anodyne, creates amorous dreams, and a powerful excitement to venery. In the adjoining chamber, his fair spouse waits, with eager expectation, to avail herself of the happy moment when her lord should awake, which is by slow degrees; and he is roused from Elysium, by her gentle offices, in tenderly embracing every part of his body, until his ideal scenes of bliss are realised; and when fully sated with the luscious banquet, they retire to the bath, to gather fresh vigour for a renewal of similar joys. In this mazy round of chaste dissipation, the hours glide gently on, and the evening is spent in dancing to the music of Pan's pipes, the flute, and *haeva* drum. They then go to the bath again, and the festivity of the evening is concluded with a repast of fruit, and young cocoanut milk. The whole village indiscriminately join the feast; and the demon of rank and precedence, with their appendages malevolence and envy, has never yet disturbed their happy board.

Happy would it have been for those people had they never been visited by Europeans; for, to our shame be it spoken, disease and gunpowder is all the benefit they have ever received from us, in return for their hospitality and kindness. The ravages of the venereal disease is evident, from the mutilated objects so frequent amongst them, where death has not thrown a charitable veil over their misery, by putting a period to their existence.

A disease of the consumptive kind has of late made great havoc amongst them; this they call the British disease, as they have only had it since their intercourse with the English.

In this complaint they are avoided by society, from a supposition of its being contagious; and in every old out-house, you will find miserable objects, for want of medical assistance, abandoned to their wretched fate. From what we could learn, it generally terminates fatally in ten or twelve months; but I am led to believe, that in many cases it originates from the venereal disease.[2]

The voice of humanity honour, and justice, calls upon us as a nation to remedy those evils, by sending some intelligent surgeon to live amongst them. They at present pant for the pruning-hand of civilization and the arts; love and adore us as beings of a superior nature, but gently upbraid us with having left them in the same abject state they were at first discovered.

We had buoyed many of them up with the hopes of carrying them to England with us, in order to secure their fidelity and honesty, especially those who were most useful in our domestic concerns; but on explaining to them that even bread was not to be obtained in England without labour, they lost hopes of their favourite voyage.

Large presents were now brought us for our sea-store; and notwithstanding Mr. Bentham our purser having most liberally supplied the ship with four pounds of fresh pork per man each day, it made no apparent scarcity; beside salting some thousand weight, and a prodigious number of goats, fowls, and other things. Could we have made it convenient to have staid another week, some cows were promised to have been sent us from a neighbouring island. Captain Cook had left with them a horse and mare, a cow with calf, and a bull; but, from some mistake, they killed a horse instead of one of the cows, and found it very tough, disagreeable eating, by which means they were disgusted with all the horned cattle, and drew an unfavourable conclusion that their meat was all of the same texture. Had some pains been taken with them, to get the better of a dislike they have to milk, and explained to them how variously it might be employed as food, I have no doubt but they would have paid more attention

2. Compare the ravages of the great Lila (wasting sickness) in Fiji, and the accounts of similar visitations following on the first visit of an European ship to an insular people. (*The Fijians*, p. 243).

to the horned cattle. They used to persist in saying that milk was urine; but on pointing to a woman that was suckling her child, and pushing their own argument, they seemed convinced of their error. We have left them a goose and a gander, which they take a great delight in.

Edea, the Queen, endeavoured to conquer that absurd dislike, and at last became fond of milk in her tea.

A painting of Captain Cook, done in oil by Webber, which had been delivered to Captain Edwards on his first landing, was now returned to them. It is held by them in the greatest veneration; and I should not be surprised if, one day or other, divine honours should be paid to it. They still believe Captain Cook is living; and their seeing Mr. Bentham our purser, whom they perfectly recollected as having been the voyage with him, and spoke their language, will confirm them in that opinion.

The harbour was surveyed by Mr. Geo. Passmore, the master, an able and experienced officer.

Our officers here, as at Rio Janeiro, showed the most manly and philanthropic disposition, by giving up their cabins, and sacrificing every comfort and convenience for the good of mankind, in accommodating boxes with plants of the Bread-fruit tree, that the laudable intentions of government might not be frustrated from the loss of his majesty's ship *Bounty*.

We had now completed our water from an excellent spring, out of a rock close to the water's edge, at Offaree.

King Ottoo, and his queen Edea, came on board, and were very importunate in their solicitations to Captain Edwards, requesting him to take them to England with him. Aeredy, the concubine, likewise requested the same favour; but she more generously begged they might all three go together. But Oripai, and the other chiefs, remonstrated against his going, as they were on the eve of a war.

We were now perfectly ready for sea; and as Captain Cook's picture is presented to all strangers, it is customary for navigators to write their observations on the back of it; so our arrival and departure was notified upon it.

The ship was filled with cocoa-nuts and fruit, as many pigs, goats, and fowls, as the decks and boats would hold. The dismal day of our departure now arrived. This I believe was the first time that an Englishman got up his anchor, at the remotest part of the globe, with a heavy heart, to go home to his own country. Every canoe almost in the island was hovering round the ship; and they began to mourn, as is customary for the death of a near relation. They bared their bodies, cut their heads with shells, and smeared their breasts and shoulders with the warm blood, as it streamed down; and as the blood ceased flowing, they renewed the wounds in their head, attended with a dismal yell.

Ottoo now took leave of us; and, with the tears trickling down his cheeks, begged to be remembered to King George. The tender was put in commission, and the command of her given to Mr. Oliver the master's mate, Mr. Renouard a midshipman, James Dodds a quartermaster; and six privates were put on board of her. She was decked, beautifully built, and the size of a Gravesend boat.

CHAPTER 2

Voyage from Otaheite
to Anamooka

With a pleasant breeze, on the evening of the 8th of May, passed Emea or York Island, contiguous to, and in sight of Otaheite. It is governed by Matuara, brother-in-law to Ottoo. It is a pleasant romantic looking spot, with very high hills upon it, and about twelve miles in circumference. They were lately attacked by some neighbouring power, and Matuara requested the lend of a musket from his friend and ally. When peace was restored, Ottoo sent for his musket. Matuara represented, that as a man, from a sense of honour, he wished to return it; but that as a king, the love he bore his subjects prevented him complying with the request. That single musket, and a few cartridges, gives him no small degree of consequence, and are retained as the royal dower of his wife.

Next morning we reached Huaheine, and sent the boats on shore in Owharre Bay. As Oedidy the chief requested to go with us to Whytutakee, he went on shore with the officers, in their search for intelligence of the mutineers; but they returned without success.

Here we learned the fate of Omai, the native of Otaheite, whom Captain Cook brought from England. On his return here he had wealth enough to obtain every fine woman on the island; and at last fell a martyr to Venus, having finished his career by the venereal disease, two years after his landing. His house and garden are still standing; but his musket occasioned a war after his death, and was found in the possession of a native of Ulitea. His servant was on board of us, but had not retained a single article of his property.

On the 10th, we examined Ulitea and Otaha, interchanged presents with the natives, and landed in Chamanen's Bay; but got no information.

We examined Bolobola on the 11th; and Tatahu, the king, honoured us with a visit. The people of this island are of a more warlike disposition than any other of the Society Islands; and on account of that national ferocity of character, are much caressed by the Otaheitans and neighbouring islands. They are sensible of their pre-eminence, and boast of their country, in whatever island you meet them. They are tattooed in a particular manner; and whether they may have spread their conquests, or other nations imitated them, I could not learn; but a prodigious number, in islands we afterwards visited, were tattooed in their fashion. What was most singular, we saw some with the glans of the penis entirely tattooed; and our men, from being tattooed in the legs, arms, and breast, places of much less sensation, were often lame for a week, from the excruciating torture of the operation. Tatahu likewise informed us there were no white men on Tubai, a small island to the northward of Bolobola, and under his jurisdiction; nor upon Mauruah, another island in sight, and to the westward of Bolobola. He also mentioned another island, which he called Mopehah. Here Oedidy went on shore; but getting drunk in meeting some of his old friends, he fell asleep, and lost his passage. On the 12th we left Mauruah, and on the 13th lost sight of the Society Islands.

Here one of the prisoners begged to speak with the captain, and gave information of Mr. Christian's intended rout.

We now shaped our course to fall in to the eastward of Whytutakee, an island discovered by Captain Bligh, and on the 19th made the island. We sent the boat on shore, covered by the tender, to examine it; but found it a thing impossible for the *Bounty* to have been there; and the natives said they had seen no white people. They were very shy, and we could not coax them on board. One of them recollected having seen Lieutenant Hayward on board the *Bounty*. Here we purchased from the natives a spear of most exquisite workmanship. It was nine feet long, and cut in the form of a Gothic spire, all its ornaments being executed in a kind of *alto relievo*; which, from the slow progress they made with stone tools, must have been the labour of a man's whole life.

Here nature begins to assume a ruder aspect; and the silken bands of love gives way to the rustic garniture of war. The natives of either sex wear no clothing, but a girdle of stained leaves round their middle, and the men a *gorget*, of the exact shape and size as at present wore by officers in our service. It is made of the pearl oyster-shell. The centre is black, and the transparent part of the shell is left as an edge or border to it, which gives it a very fine effect. It is slung round their neck with a band of human hair, or the fibres of cocoa nut-shell, of admirable texture, and a rose worked at each corner of the *gorget*, the same as the military jemmy of the present day.

We now began to discover, that the ladies of Otaheite had left us many warm tokens of their affection.

Instructions were given to the commander of the tender to be particular in guarding against surprise, and a rendezvous established, in case of separation; and on Sunday, the 22nd of May, made Palmerston's Islands.

The tender's signal was made to cover the boats in landing; and some natives were seen rowing across the lagoon to a considerable distance. Soon after their landing, Lieutenant Corner and his party discovered a yard and some spars marked *Bounty*, and the broad arrow upon them. When this intelligence was communicated to the ship, a signal was made to the party on shore to advance with great circumspection, and to guard against surprise. Mr. Rickards, the master's mate, went in the cutter, and made a circuit of the island.

Lieutenants Corner and Hayward landed on the different isles with cork-jackets; but the surf running very high all round, rendered it exceedingly dangerous, and in many places impracticable. Had they not been expert swimmers, in duty of this kind, they must have certainly been drowned, as they had not only themselves and the party to take care of, but the arms and ammunition to land dry.

About four o'clock in the afternoon, Mr. Sival the midshipman came on board in the jolly-boat, and brought with him several very curious stained canoes, representing the figure of men, fishes, and beasts. He had committed some mistake in the orders he was sent to execute, and was ordered to return immediately to rectify it; but the boat did not come back again. A few minutes after she left the ship, the weather became thick and hazy, and began to blow fresh; so that, even with the assistance of glasses, they could not see whether she made the shore or not. It continued to blow during the night, so as to prevent the party on shore from coming on board. They had been employed during the day in searching all the islands with particular attention, having every reason to suspect the mutineers were there, from finding the *Bounty's* yard and spars. But at last, wore out with fatigue in marching, and swimming through so many reefs, and having no victuals the whole day, in the evening they began to forage for something to eat. The gigantic cockle was the only thing that presented. Of the shell of one they made a kettle, to boil some junks of it in. (It may be necessary here to remark, for the information of those who are not acquainted with it, that there are some of them larger than three men can carry.) Of this coarse fare, and some cocoa-nuts, they made shift, with the assistance of a good appetite, to make a tolerable hearty supper; they then set the watch, and went to sleep. They had thrown a large nut on the fire before they lay down, and forgot it; but in the middle of the night, the milk of the cocoa-nut became so expanded with the heat, that it burst with a great explosion. Their minds had been so much engaged in the course of the day with the enterprise they were employed in, expecting muskets to be fired at them from every bush, that they all jumped up, seized their arms, and were some time before they could undeceive themselves that they were really not attacked.

In the morning the boats returned; and we were much concerned to hear that they had seen nothing of the jolly-boat. The tender received a fresh supply of provisions and ammunition; at the same time they had orders to cruise in a certain direction, to look for the jolly-boat; and Palmerston's Isles was appointed as a rendezvous to meet again. Lieutenant Corner now came on board, in a canoe not much bigger than a butcher's tray. The cutter was sent a second time to search the reefs, but returned without success. We then run down with the ship in the direction the wind had blown the preceding day, in hopes of finding the boat; but after a whole day's run to leeward, and working up again by traverses to the isles, saw nothing of her. The tender hove in sight in the evening, and we again searched the isles without success. All further hopes of seeing her were given up, and we proceeded on our voyage. It may be difficult to surmise what has been the fate of these unfortunate men. They had a piece of salt-beef thrown into the boat to them on leaving the ship; and it rained a good deal that night and the following day, which might satiate their thirst. It is by these accidents the Divine Ruler of the universe has peopled the southern hemisphere.[1]

Here are innumerable islands in perpetual growth. The coral, a marine vegetable, with which the South Seas in every part abounds, is continually shooting up from the bottom to the surface, which at first forms lagoon islands; and the water in the centre is evaporated by the heat of the sun, till at last a terra firma is completed. In this state it would for ever remain a barren sand, had not Divine Providence given birth to the cocoanut tree, whose fruit is so protected with a hard shell, that after floating about for a twelve-month in the sea, it will vegetate, take root, and grow in those salt marshes, lagoons, incipient islands, or what you please to call them. Their roots serve to bind

---

1. This gives occasion for a splenetic and unjust tirade from an anonymous writer in the *United Service Journal* for 1831: "When this boat with a midshipman and several men (four) had been inhumanely ordered from alongside, it was known that there was nothing in her but one piece of salt beef, compassionately thrown in by a seaman; and horrid as must have been their fate, the flippant surgeon, after detailing the disgraceful fact, adds 'that this is the way the world was peopled,' or words to that effect, for we quote only from memory." With a fresh E.S.E. breeze and no provisions there can be little doubt that Midshipman Sival perished at sea, but neither Edwards nor Hamilton are to be censured, the former for despatching a boat on ordinary duty, the latter for penning a platitude.

the surface of the coral; and the annual shedding of their leaves, in time creates a soil which produces a verdure or undergrowth. This affords a favourite resting-place to sea-fowls, and the whole feathered race, who in their dung drop the seeds of shrubs, fruits, and plants; by which means all the variety of the vegetable kingdom is disseminated. At last the variegated landscape rises to the view; and when the divine Architect has finished his work, it becomes then a residence for man.

From the various accidents incident to man in the early stages of society, their wants, and the restless spirit inherent in their natures, they are tempted to dare the elements, either in fishing, commerce, or war; and from their temerity are often blown to remote and uninhabited islands. Distressing accidents of this nature often happening to inhabitants of the South Seas, they now seldom undertake any hazardous enterprise by water without a woman, and a sow with pig, being in the canoe with them; by which means, if they are cast on any of those uninhabited islands, they fix their abode.

Their remote situation from European powers has deprived them of the culture of civilised life, as they neither serve to swell the ambitious views of conquest, nor the avarice of commerce. Here the sacred finger of Omnipotence has interposed, and rendered our vices the instruments of virtue; and although that unfortunate man Christian has, in a rash unguarded moment, been tempted to swerve from his duty to his king and country, as he is in other respects of an amiable character and respectable abilities, should he elude the hand of justice, it may be hoped he will employ his talents in humanizing the rude savages; so that, at some future period, a British Ilion may blaze forth in the south with all the characteristic virtues of the English nation, and complete the great prophecy, by propagating the Christian knowledge amongst the infidels. As Christian has taken fourteen beautiful women with him from Otaheite, there is little doubt of his intention of colonising some undiscovered island.

On the 6th day of June, we discovered an island, which was named the Duke of York's Island. Lieutenants Corner and Hayward were sent out to examine it in the two yawls, covered by the tender. Some huts being discovered by the ship, a signal was immediately made for the party on shore to be on their guard, and to advance with caution.

Soon after their arrival on shore, a ship's wooden buoy was discovered. On searching the huts, nets of different sizes were found hanging in them, and a variety of fishing utensils. Stages and wharfs were likewise discovered in different parts of the creek, which led us to imagine it was only an island resorted to in the fishing season by some neighbouring nation. The skeleton of a very large fish, supposed to be a whale, was found near the beach; and a place of venerable aspect, formed entirely by the hand of Nature, and resembling a Druidical temple, commanded their attention. The falling of a very large old tree, formed an arch, through which the interior part of the temple was seen, which heightened the perspective, and gave a romantic solemn dignity to the scene. At the extreme end of the temple, three altars were placed, the centre one higher than the other two, on which some white shells were piled in regular order.[2]

After traversing the island, they returned to the huts, and hung up a few knives, looking-glasses, and some little articles of European manufacture, that the natives, on their return, might know the island had been visited.

On the 12th, we discovered another island, which was named the Duke of Clarence's island. In running along the land, we saw several canoes crossing the lagoons. The tender's signal was made, to cover the boats in landing, and Lieutenants Corner and Hayward sent to reconnoitre the beach, to discover a landing-place. In this duty they came pretty near some of the natives in their canoes, who made signs of peace to them; but, either from fear or business, avoided having any intercourse with us. *Morais*, or burying-places, were likewise found here, which indicated it to be a principal residence. Here they find some old cocoa trees hollowed longitudinally, as tanks or reservoirs for the rain water.

---

2. This suggests the Fijian *Nanga*, or 'bed of the ancestors,' a cult introduced by native castaways many generations ago. These castaways may have been Polynesians.

On the 18th, we discovered an island of more considerable extent than any island that has hitherto been discovered in the south; and as there were many collateral circumstances which might hereafter promise it to be a discovery of national importance, in honour of the first lord of the admiralty, it was called Chatham's Island. It is beautifully diversified with hills and dales, of twice the extent of Otaheite, and a hardy warlike race of people. The natives described a large river to us, which disembogued itself into a spacious bay, that promises excellent anchorage.[3] Here we learned the death of Fenow, king of Anamooka, from one of his family of the same name, who had a finger cut off in mourning for him. After trading a whole day with the natives, who seemed fair and honourable in their dealings, we examined it without success, and proceeded on our voyage.

On the 21st we discovered a very considerable island, of about forty miles long. It was named by the natives Otutuelah. Captain Edwards gave no name to it; but should posterity derive the advantages from it which it at present promises, I presume it may hereafter be called Edwards's Island.[4]

It is well wooded with immense large trees, whose foliage spreads like the oak; and there is a deal of shrubbery on it, bearing a yellow flower. The natives are remarkably handsome. Some of them had their skins tinged with yellow, as a mark of distinction, which at first led us to imagine they were diseased. Neither sex wear any clothing but a girdle of leaves round their middle, stained with different colours. The women adorn their hair with chaplets of sweet-smelling flowers and bracelets, and necklaces of flowers round their wrists and neck.

On their first coming on board, they trembled for fear. They were perfectly ignorant of fire-arms, never having seen a European ship before. They made many gestures of submission, and were struck with wonder and surprise at every thing they saw. Amongst other things, they brought us some most remarkable fine puddings, which abounded with aromatic spiceries, that excelled in taste and flavour the most delicate seed-cake. As we

---

3. Savaii in the Samoa group. See p. 49 *ante*.
4. It is known by its native name, Tutuila.

have never hitherto known of spices or aromatics being in the South Seas, it is certainly a matter worthy the investigation of some future circumnavigators. We traded with them the whole day, and got many curiosities. Birds and fowls, of the most splendid plumage, were brought on board, some resembling the peacock, and a great variety of the parrot kind.

One woman amongst many others came on board. She was six feet high, of exquisite beauty, and exact symmetry, being naked, and unconscious of her being so, added a lustre to her charms; for, in the words of the poet, "She needed not the foreign ornaments of dress; careless of beauty, she was beauty's self."

Many mouths were watering for her; but Captain Edwards, with great humanity and prudence, had given previous orders, that no woman should be permitted to go below, as our health had not quite recovered the shock it received at Otaheite; and the lady was obliged to be contented with viewing the great cabin, where she was shown the wonders of the Lord on the face of the mighty deep. Before evening, the women went all on shore, and the men began to be troublesome and pilfering. The third lieutenant had a new coat stole out of his cabin; and they were making off with every bit of iron they could lay hands on.

It now came on to blow fresh, and we were obliged to make off from the land. Those who were engaged in trade on board were so anxious, that we had got almost out of sight of their canoes before they perceived the ship's motion, when they all jumped into the water like a flock of wild geese; but one fellow, more earnest than the rest, hung by the rudder chains for a mile or two, thinking to detain her.

This evening, at five o'clock, we unfortunately parted company, and lost sight of our tender. False fires were burnt, and great guns and small arms were fired without success, as it came on thick blowing weather.

We cruised for her all the 23rd and 24th, near where we parted company, which was off a piece of remarkable high land. What was most unfortunate, water and provisions were then on deck for her, which were intended to have been put on board of her in the morning. She had the day before received orders, in case of separation, to rendezvous at Anamooka, and to wait there for us. A small keg of salt, and another of nails and iron-ware, were likewise put on board of her, to traffic with the Indians, and the latitudes and longitudes of the places we would touch at, in our intended rout. She had a boarding netting fixed, to prevent her being boarded, and several seven-barrelled pieces and blunderbusses put on board of her.

As we proceeded to the eastward, we saw another island, which we knew to be one of the navigator's isles, discovered by Mons. Bougainville. On the 28th, in the morning, saw the Happy Islands, discovered by Captain Cook, and before noon, the group of islands to the eastward of Anamooka, and sailed down between Little Anamooka and the Fallafagee Island.

On the 29th, we anchored in the road of Anamooka. Immediately on our arrival, a large sailing canoe was hired, and Lieutenant Hayward and one private sent to the Happai and Feegee Islands,[5] to make inquiry after the *Bounty* and our tender; but received no intelligence. Here they found an axe, which had been left by Captain Cook, and bartered with the natives of the different islands for hogs, yams, &c.

The people of Anamooka are the most daring set of robbers in the South Seas; and, with the greatest deference and submission to Captain Cook, I think the name of Friendly Isles is a perfect misnomer, as their behaviour to himself, to us, and to Captain Bligh's unfortunate boat at Murderer's Cove, pretty clearly evinces. Indeed Murderer's Cove, in the Friendly Isles, is saying a volume on the subject.

Two or three of the officers were taking a walk on shore one evening, who had the precaution to take their pistols with them. They seemed to crowd round us with more than idle curiosity; but, on presenting the pistols to them, they sheered off. The captain soon joined us, and brought his servant with him, carrying a bag of nails, and some trifling presents, which he meant to distribute amongst them; but he took the bag from him, and dispatched him with a message to the boat, on which the crowd followed him. As soon as he got out of our sight, they stripped

5. A mistake. Hayward visited Huapai only.

him naked, and robbed him of his clothes, and every article he had, but one shoe, which he used for concealing his nakedness. At this juncture Lieutenant Hayward arrived from his expedition, and called the assistance of the guard in searching for the robbers. We saw the natives all running, and dodging behind the trees, which led us to suspect there was some mischief brewing; but we soon discovered the great Irishman, with his shoe full in one hand, and a bayonet in the other, naked and foaming mad with revenge on the natives, for the treatment he had received. Night coming on, we went on board, without recovering the poor fellow's clothes.

Next day we were honoured with a visit from Tatafee, king of Anamooka, who was of lineal descent from the same family that reigned in the island when discovered by Tasman, the Dutch circumnavigator; and the story of his landing and supplying them with dogs and hogs, is handed down, by oral tradition, to this day.[6]

Here society may be said to exist in the second stage with respect to Otaheite. As land is scarcer, private property is more exactly ascertained, and each man's possession fenced in with a beautiful Chinese railing. Highways, and roads leading to public places, are neatly fenced in on each side, and a handsome approach to their houses by a gravel-walk, with shrubbery planted with some degree of taste on each side of it. Many of them had rows of pine apples on each side of the avenue. Messrs. Hayward and Corner, with their usual benevolence, took much pains in teaching them the manner of transplanting their pine-apples; which hint they immediately adopted, and were very thankful for any advice, either in rearing their fruit, or cultivating their ground. The shaddocks are superior in flavour to those of the West Indies; and they will soon have oranges from what we have left amongst them.

The women here are extremely beautiful; and although they want that feminine softness of manners which the Otaheite women possess in so eminent a degree, their matchless vivacity, and fine animated countenances, compensate the want of the softer blandishments of their sister island.

---

6. Tasman visited Namuka in 1642.

There is a favourite amusement of the ladies here, (the cup and ball), such as children play at in England. It serves to give them a *dégagé* kind of air, by which means you have a more elegant display of their charms. They are well aware of their fascinating powers, and use them with as much address as our fine women do knotting, and other acts of industry. Trade went briskly on. They brought abundance of hogs, and several ton weight of very excellent yams. We found that the pork took salt, and was cured much better here than at Otaheite.

Many beautiful girls were brought on board for sale by their mothers, who were very exorbitant in their demands, as nothing less than a broad axe would satisfy them; but after standing their market three days, *la pucelage* fell to an old razor, a pair of scissors, or a very large nail. Indeed this trade was pushed to so great a height, that the quarter-deck became the scene of the most indelicate familiarities. Nor did the unfeeling mothers commiserate with the pain and suffering of the poor girls, but seemed to enjoy it as a monstrous good thing. It is customary here, when girls meet with an accident of this kind, that a council of matrons is held, and the noviciate has a gash made in her fore finger. We soon observed a number of cut fingers amongst them; and had the razors held out, I believe all the girls in the island would have undergone the same operation.

A party was sent on shore to cut wood for fuel, and grass for the sheep; but they would not permit a blade of grass to be cut till they were paid for it.

The watering party shared the same fate; and notwithstanding a guard of armed men were sent to protect the others whilst on that duty, the natives were continually harassing them, and committing depredations. One of them came behind Lieutenant Corner, and made a blow at him with his club, which luckily missed his head, and only stunned him in the back of the neck; and, while in that state, snatched his handkerchief from him; but Mr. Corner recovering before the thief got out of sight, levelled his piece and shot him dead.

Tatafee[7] the king was going to collect tribute from the is-

7. Fatafehi.

lands under his jurisdiction, and went in the frigate to Tofoa; but previous to our sailing, a letter was left to Mr. Oliver, the commander of the tender, should he chance to arrive before our return, with Macaucala, a principal chief. In the night, the burning mountain on Tofoa exhibited a very grand spectacle; and in the morning two canoes were sent on shore, to announce the arrival of those two great personages, Tatafee and Toobou, who went on shore in the *Pandora*'s barge, to give them more consequence; but the tributary princes came off in canoes, to do homage to Tatafee before he reached the shore. They came alongside the barge, lowered their heads over the side of the canoe, and Tatafee, agreeable to their custom, put his foot upon their heads. When on shore, what presents he had received from us, he distributed amongst his subjects, with a liberality worthy of a great prince.

Some of the people were here who behaved with such savage barbarity to Captain Bligh's boat at Murderer's Cove. They perfectly recollected Mr. Hayward, and seemed to shrink from him. Captain Edwards took much pains with Tatafee, the king, to make him sensible of his disapprobation of their conduct to Captain Bligh's boat. But conciliatory and gentle means were all that could be enjoined at present, lest our tender should fall in amongst them.

CHAPTER 3

The Loss of the *Pandora*

The wind not permitting us to visit Tongataboo, we proceeded to Catooa and Navigator's Isles, the loss of our tender
having prevented us from doing it before, and endeavoured to
fall in with the easternmost of these islands.

On the morning of the 12th of July, we discovered a cluster
of islands in the N.W. quarter; but the wind being favourable for
us, left examining of them till our return to the Friendly Isles.[1]
On the 14th, in the forenoon, saw three isles, supposed to be
the cluster of isles called by Bougainville Navigator's Isles. The
largest the natives called Tumaluah.[2] We passed them at a little
distance, and found much entreaty necessary to bring them on
board.

On the 15th, we saw another island, which proved to be
Otutuelah,[3] which has been already described. Here we found
some of the French navigator's clothing and buttons; and there
is little doubt but they have murdered them.[4]

On the 18th, saw the group of islands we discovered on our
way here; and on the 19th, ran down the north side till we came
to an opening, where we saw the sea on the other side. A sound
is formed here by some islands to the south east and north west,
and interior bays, which promises better anchorage than any
other place in the Friendly Isles. The natives told us there were

1. Vavau.
2. Manua.
3. Tutuila.
4. De Langle's boat had been cut off on 10 Dec. 1787.

excellent watering-places in several different parts within the sound. The country is well wooded. Several of the inferior chiefs were on board, one of the Tatafee, and one of the Toobou family; but the principal chief was not on board. We supposed he was coming off just as we sailed.[5] The natives in general were very fair and honourable in their dealings. They were more inoffensive and better behaved than any we had seen for some time. They have frequent intercourse with Anamooka, and their religion, customs, and language, are the same.

A number of beautiful parakeets were brought off by the natives, all remarkable for the richness and variety of their plumage.

The group of islands was called Howe's Islands, but were particularly distinguished by the names of Barrington's, Sawyer's, Hotham's, and Jarvis's Islands. The sound itself was called Curtis's Sound. Under the general denomination of Howe's Islands, were included several islands to the south east, to which we gave no particular name, and two more islands to the westward, called Bickerton's Islands, including two small islands near the above. There seems to be a tolerable landing-place on the north-west side of Gardner's Island. All this part of the island has a most barren aspect. There were evident marks of volcanic eruptions having happened. The very singular appearance which this part of the island presented, I cannot omit mentioning; it bore the figure of a piece of flat table-land, without the slightest eminence or indentation, and smoke was issuing from the edges, round its whole circumference.

On the 23rd, we passed an inhabited island, which we supposed to be the Pylestaart island. It has two remarkable high peaks upon it.

On the 26th, we saw Middleburg Island, and run down between it and Euah; examined it without success; passed Tongatabu; got some provisions here, but found the water brackish.

On the 29th, we anchored again in the road of Anamooka. We were sorry to hear the tender had not been there. On the 5th of August, we again proceeded on our voyage. As the occurrences at this time bore some semblance to the transactions

---

5. Finau Ulukalala.

in our last visit, to avoid wounding the delicate, or satiating the licentious, we shall conclude in the torpid phraseology of the log, with ditto repeated.

Every thing being ready for sea on the 3rd day of August, we sailed from Anamooka; and on the 5th, discovered an island of some considerable extent, called by the natives Onooafow,[6] which we called Proby's Island, in honour of Commissioner Proby. We traded with the inhabitants for some hours. The land was hilly, and the houses of much larger construction than we had observed in those seas.

We were now convinced that we were further to the westward than we imagined, and therefore shaped a course to fall in to the eastward of Wallis's Island; and next day fell in with it. We gave presents, as customary, to the first boat; who, from a theft they committed, were afraid to return. Their cheek-bones were much bruised and flattened, and some had both their little fingers cut off.[7]

We bore away, intending to steer in the track of Carteret and Bligh, between Spirito Santo and Santa Cruz; and on the 8th saw land to the westward. We sounded, but found no bottom. We run down the island, and saw a vast number of houses amongst the trees. It is very hilly, and, from the great height of some of them, may be called mountains. They are cultivated to the top; the reason of which, I presume, is from its being so full of inhabitants. It is about seven miles long; and being a new discovery, we called it Grenville's Island, in honour of Lord Grenville. The name the natives gave it is Rotumah. They came off in a fleet of canoes, rested on their paddles, and gave the war-hoop at stated periods. They were all armed with clubs, and meant to attack us; but the magnitude and novelty of such an object as a man of war, struck them with a mixture of wonder and fear. They were, however, perfectly ignorant of fire-arms, and seemed much startled at the report of a musket, were too shy to stand the experiment of a great gun. As they came off with hostile intentions, they brought no women with them.

6. Niuafoou.
7. A sign of mourning.

They wore necklaces, bracelets, and girdles of white shells. Their bodies were curiously marked with the figures of men, dogs, fishes, and birds, upon every part of them; so that every man was a moving landscape. These marks were all raised, and done, I suppose, by pinching up the skin.

They were great adepts in thieving, and uncommonly athletic and strong. One fellow was making off with some booty, but was detected; and although five of the stoutest men in the ship were hanging upon him, and had fast hold of his long flowing black hair, he overpowered them all, and jumped overboard with his prize. There is a high promontory on this island, which we named Mount Temple.

On the 11th, no land being then in sight, we run over a reef of coral, in eleven fathom water. We were much alarmed, but passed it in five minutes; and on sounding immediately afterwards, found no bottom. This was called *Pandora's* Reef.

On the 12th, in the morning, we discovered an island well wooded, but not inhabited. It had two remarkable promontories on it, one resembling a mitre, and the other a steeple; from whence we called it Mitre Island. We passed it, and stood to the westward; and at ten, the same morning, discovered another island to the north west. It is entirely cultivated, and a vast number of inhabitants, though only a mile in length. The beach from the east, round by the south, is a white sand, but too much surf for a boat to attempt to land. In gratitude for the many good things we had on board, and the very high state of preservation in which they kept, we called this Cherry's Island, in honour of —— Cherry, Esq; commissioner of the victualling-office.[8]

On the 13th of August, we discovered another island to the north west. It is mountainous, and covered with wood to the very summit. We saw no inhabitants, but smoke in many different parts of it, from which it may be presumed it is inhabited. This we called Pitt's Island.[9]

On the 17th, at midnight, we discovered breakers on each bow. We had just room to wear ship; and as this merciful escape

---

8. Anula.
9. Vanikoro.

was from the vigilance of one Wells, who was looking out ahead, it was called Wells's Shoals. Those hair-breadth escapes may point out the propriety of a consort. In the morning, at daylight, we put about, to examine the danger we were in, and found we had got embayed in a double reef, which will very soon be an island. We run round its north west end, and on the 23rd saw land, which we supposed to be the Luisiade, a cape bearing north east and by east. We called it Cape Rodney. Another contiguous to it was called Cape Hood; and a mountain between them, we named Mount Clarence.

After passing Cape Hood, the land appears lower, and to trench away about north west, forming a deep bay; and it may be doubted whether it joins New Guinea or not.

We pursued our course to the westward, keeping Endeavour Straits open, by which means we hoped to avoid the dangers Captain Cook met with in higher latitudes.

On the 25th, saw breakers; hauled up, and passed to the westward of them; the sea broke very gently on them. To these we gave the name of Look-out Shoals. Before noon we saw more breakers, the reef of which was composed of very large stones, and called it Stony-reef Island.

On seeing obstruction to the southward, stood to the westward, where there appeared to be an opening. We saw an island in that direction, and a reef extending a considerable way to the north west. Hauled upon the wind, seeing our passage obstructed, and stood off and on, under an easy sail in the night, till daylight; and in the morning bore away, and discovered four islands, to which the name of Murray's Islands was given. On the top of the largest, there was something resembling a fortification. We saw at the same time three two-masted boats. We kept running along the reef, and in the forenoon thought we saw an opening. Lieutenant Corner was immediately ordered to get ready, to discover if there was a passage for the ship, and went to the topmasthead, to look well round him before he left us. It was judged necessary that he should take with him an axe, some fuel, provisions, a little water, and a compass, previous to his departure.

It was now the 28th of August. It had lately been our custom to lay to in the night, M. Bougainville having represented this part of the ocean as exceedingly dangerous; and it certainly is the boldest piece of navigation that has ever yet been attempted. We would gladly have continued the same custom; but the great length of the voyage would not permit it, as, after we had passed to the westward of Bougainville's track, the ocean was perfectly unexplored.

At five in the afternoon, a signal was made from the boat, that a passage through the reef was discovered for the ship; but wishing to be well informed in so intricate a business, and the day being far spent, we waited the boats coming on board, made a signal to expedite her, and afterwards repeated it. Night closing fast upon us, and considering our former misfortunes of losing the tender and jolly-boat, rendered it necessary, both for the preservation of the boat, and the success of the voyage, to endeavour, by every possible means, to get hold of her.

False fires were burnt, and muskets fired from the ship, and answered by the boat reciprocally; and as the flashes from their muskets were distinctly seen by us, she was reasonably soon expected on board. We now sounded, but had no bottom with a hundred and ten fathom line, till past seven o'clock, when we got ground in fifty fathom. The boat was now seen close under the stern; we were at the same time lying to, to prevent the ship fore-reaching. Immediately on sounding this last time, the topsails were filled; but before the tacks were hauled on board, and the sails trimmed, she struck on a reef of rocks, and at that instant the boat got on board. Every possible effort was attempted to get her off by the sails; but that failing, they were furled, and the boats hoisted out with a view to carry out an anchor. Before that was accomplished, the carpenter reported she made eighteen inches water in five minutes; and in a quarter of an hour more, she had nine feet water in the hold.

The hands were immediately turned to the pumps, and to bale at the different hatchways. Some of the prisoners were let out of irons, and turned to the pumps. At this dreadful crisis, it blew very violently; and she beat so hard upon the rocks, that we expected her, every minute, to go to pieces. It was an exceeding dark, stormy night; and the gloomy horrors of death presented us all round, being every where encompassed with rocks, shoals, and broken water. About ten she beat over the reef; and we let go the anchor in fifteen fathom water.

The guns were ordered to be thrown overboard; and what hands could be spared from the pumps, were employed thrumbing a topsail to haul under her bottom, to endeavour to fodder her. To add to our distress, at this juncture one of the chain-pumps gave way; and she gained fast upon us. The scheme of the topsail was now laid aside, and every soul fell to baling and pumping. All the boats, excepting one, were obliged to keep a long distance off on account of the broken water, and the very high surf that was running near us. We baled between life and death; for had she gone down before day-light, every soul must have perished. She now took a heel, and some of the guns they were endeavouring to throw over board run down to leeward, which crushed one man to death; about the same time, a spare topmast came down from the booms, and killed another man.

The people now became faint at the pumps, and it was necessary to give them some refreshment. We had luckily between decks a cask of excellent strong ale, which we brewed at Anamooka. This was tapped, and served regularly to all hands, which was much preferable to spirits, as it gave them strength without intoxication. During this trying occasion, the men behaved with the utmost intrepidity and obedience, not a man flinching from his post. We continually cheered them at the pumps with the delusive hopes of its being soon day-light.

About half an hour before day-break, a council of war was held amongst the officers; and as she was then settling fast down in the water, it was their unanimous opinion, that nothing further could be done for the preservation of his Majesty's ship; and it was their next care to save the lives of the crew. To effect which, spars, booms, hen-coops, and every thing buoyant was cut loose, that when she went down, they might chance to get hold of something. The prisoners were ordered to be let out of irons. The water was now coming faster in at the gun-ports than the pumps could discharge; and to this minute the men never swerved from their duty. She now took a very heavy heel, so much that she lay quite down on one side.

One of the officers now told the captain, who was standing aft, that the anchor on our bow was under water; that she was then going; and, bidding him farewell, jumped over the quarter into the water. The captain then followed his example, and jumped after him. At that instant she took her last heel; and, while every one were scrambling to windward, she sunk in an instant. The crew had just time to leap over board, accompanying it with a most dreadful yell. The cries of the men drowning in the water was at first awful in the extreme; but as they sunk, and became faint, it died away by degrees. The boats, who were at some considerable distance in the drift of the tide, in about half an hour, or little better, picked up the remainder of our wretched crew.

Morning now dawned, and the sun shone out. A sandy key, four miles off, and about thirty paces long, afforded us a resting place; and when all the boats arrived, we mustered our remains, and found that thirty-five men and four prisoners were drowned.

After we had a little recovered our strength, the first care was to haul up the boats. A guard was placed over the prisoners. Providentially a small barrel of water, a keg of wine, some biscuit, and a few muskets and *cartouche* boxes, had been thrown into the boat. The heat of the sun, and the reflection from the sand, was now excruciating; and our stomachs being filled with salt water, from the great length of time we were swimming before we were picked up, rendered our thirst most intolerable; and no water was allowed to be served out the first day. By a calculation which we made, by filling the compass boxes, and every utensil we had, we could admit an allowance of two small wine glasses of water a-day to each man for sixteen days.

A saw and hammer had fortunately been in one of the boats, which enabled us, with the greater expedition, to make preparations for our voyage, by repairing one of the boats, which was in a very bad state, and cutting up the floor-boards of all the boats into uprights, round which we stretched canvas, to keep the water from breaking into the boats at sea. We made tents of the boats' sails; and when it was dark, we set the watch, and went to sleep. In the night we were disturbed by the irregular behaviour of one Connell, which led us to suspect he had stole our wine, and got drunk; but, on further inquiry, we found that the excruciating torture he suffered from thirst led him to drink salt water; by which means he went mad, and died in the sequel of the voyage.

Next morning Mr. George Passmore, the master, was dispatched in one of the boats to visit the wreck, to see if any thing floated round her that might be useful to us in our present distressed state. He returned in two hours, and brought with him a cat, which he found clinging to the top-gallant-mast-head; a piece of the top-gallant-mast, which he cut away; and about fifteen feet of the lightning chain; which being copper, we cut up, and converted into nails for fitting out the boats. Some of the gigantic cockle was boiled, and cut into junks, lest any one should be inclined to eat. But our thirst was too excessive to bear any thing which would increase it. This evening a wine glass of water was served to each man. A paper parcel of tea having been thrown into the boat, the officers joined all their allowance, and had tea in the captain's tent with him. When it was boiled, every one took a salt-cellar spoonful, and passed it to his neighbour; by which means we moistened our mouths by slow degrees, and received much refreshment from it.

CHAPTER 4

From the Wreck to Timor

Every thing being ready on the following day, at twelve o'clock, we embarked in our little squadron, each boat having been previously supplied with the latitude and longitude of the island of Timor, eleven hundred miles from this place.

Our order of sailing was as follows. In the pinnace: Captain Edwards, Lieutenant Hayward, Mr. Rickards, master's mate, Mr. Packer, gunner, Mr. Edmonds, captain's clerk, 3 prisoners, 16 privates. In the red yawl: Lieutenant Larkan, Mr. Geo. Hamilton, surgeon, Mr. Reynolds, master's mate, Mr. Matson, midshipman, 2 prisoners, 18 privates. In the launch: Lieutenant Corner, Mr. Gregory Bentham, Purser, Mr. Montgomery, carpenter, Mr. Bowling, master's mate, Mr. M'Kendrick, midshipman, 2 prisoners, 24 privates. In the blue yawl: Mr. Geo. Passmore, master, Mr. Cunningham, boatswain, Mr. James Innes, surgeon's mate, Mr. Fenwick, midshipman, Mr. Pycroft, midshipman, 3 prisoners, 15 privates.

As soon as embarked, we laid the oars upon the thwarts, which formed a platform, by which means we stowed two tier of men. A pair of wooden scales was made in each boat, and a musket-ball weight of bread served to each man. At meridian we saw a key, bounded with large craggy rocks. As the principal part of our subsistence was in the launch, it was necessary to keep together, both for our defence and support. We towed each other during the night, and at day-break cast off the tow-line.

At eight in the morning, the red and blue yawls were sent ahead, to sound and investigate the coast of New South Wales, and to search for a watering-place. The country had been described as very destitute of the article of water; but on entering a very fine bay, we found most excellent water rushing from a spring at the very edge of the beach. Here we filled our bellies, a tea-kettle, and two quart bottles. The pinnace and launch had gone too far ahead to observe any signal of our success; and immediately we made sail after them. The coast has a very barren aspect; and, from the appearance of the soil and land, looks like a country abounding with minerals.

As we passed round the bay, two canoes, with three black men in each, put off, and paddled very hard to get near us. They stood up in the canoes, waved, and made many signs for us to come to them. But as they were perfectly naked, had a very savage aspect, and having heard an indifferent account of the natives of that country, we judged it prudent to avoid them.

In two hours we joined the pinnace and launch, who were lying to for us. At ten at night we were alarmed with the dreadful cry of breakers ahead. We had got amongst a reef of rocks; and in our present state, being worn out and fatigued, it is difficult to say how we got out of them, as the place was fraught with danger all round; for in standing clear of Scylla, we might fall foul of Charybdis; the horror of which, considering our present situation, may be better understood than expressed. After running along, we came to an inhabited island, from which we promised ourselves a supply of water. On our approach, the natives flocked down to the beach in crowds. They were jet black, and neither sex had either covering or girdle. We made signals of distress to them for something to drink, which they understood; and on receiving some trifling presents of knives, and some buttons cut off our coats, they brought us a keg of good water, which we emptied in a minute, and then sent it back to be filled again. They, however, would not bring it the second time, but put it down on the beach, and made signs to us to come on shore for it. This we declined, as we observed the women and children running, and supplying the men with bows and arrows. In a few minutes, they let fly a shower of arrows amongst the thick of us. Luckily we had not a man wounded; but an arrow fell between the captain and third lieutenant, and went through the boats thwart, and stuck in it. It was an oak-plank inch thick. We immediately discharged a volley of muskets at them, which put them to flight. There were, however, none of them killed. We now abandoned all hopes of refreshment here. This island lies contiguous to Mountainous Island.

It may be observed, that the channel throughout the reef is better than any hitherto known. We ascertained the latitudes with the greatest accuracy and exactness; and should government be inclined to plant trees on those sandy keys, particularly the outermost one, it would be a good distinguishing mark; and many difficulties which Captain Cook experienced to the southward would also be avoided. The cocoa-nut tree, on account of its hardy nature, and the Norfolk and common pines, might be preferred, from their height rendering the place more conspicuous. The tides or currents are strong and irregular here, as may be expected, from the extending reefs, shoals, and keys, and its vicinity to Endeavour Straits.

We steered from these hostile savages to other islands in sight, and sent some armed men on shore, with orders to keep pretty near us, and to run close along shore in the boats. But they returned without success. This island we called Plumb Island, from its bearing an austere, astringent kind of fruit, resembling plumbs, but not fit to eat.

In the evening, we steered for those islands which we supposed were called the Prince of Wales's Islands; and about two o'clock in the morning, came to an anchor with a grappling, along side of an island, which we called Laforey's Island. As the night was very dark, and this was the last land that could afford us relief, all hands went to sleep, to refresh our woe-worn spirits.

The morning was ushered in with the howling of wolves, who had smelt us in the night, when prowling for food. Lieutenant Corner and a party were sent at day-light, to search again for water; and, as we approached, the wild beasts retired, and filled the woods with their hideous growling. As soon as we landed, we discovered a foot-path which led down into a hollow, where we were led to suspect that water might be found; and on digging four or five feet, we had the ecstatic pleasure to see a spring rush out. A glad messenger was immediately dispatched to the beach, to make a signal to the boats of our success. On traversing the shore, we discovered a *morai*, or rather a heap of bones. There were amongst them two human skulls, the bones of some large animals, and some turtle-bones. They were heaped together in the form of a grave, and a very long paddle, supported at each end by a bifurcated branch of a tree, was laid horizontally along it.

Near to this, there were marks of a fire having been recently made. The ground about was much footed and wore; whence it may be presumed feasts or sacrifices had been frequently held, as there were several foot-paths which led to this spot. After having gorged our parched bodies with water, till we were perfectly water-logged, we began to feel the cravings of hunger; a new sensation of misery we had hitherto been strangers to, from the excess of thirst predominating. Some of our stragglers were lucky enough to find a few small oysters on the shore. A harsh, austere, astringent kind of fruit, resembling a plumb, was found in some places. As I discovered some to be pecked at by the birds, we permitted the men to fill their bellies with them. There was a small berry, of a similar taste to the plumb, which was found by some of the party. On observing the dung of some of the larger animals, many of them were found in it, in an undigested state; we therefore concluded we might venture upon them with safety. We carefully avoided shooting at any bird, lest the report of the muskets should alarm the natives, whom we had every reason to suspect were at no great distance, from the number of foot paths that led over the hill, and the noise we heard at intervals. Sentinels were placed to prevent stragglers of our party from exceeding the proper bounds; and when every other thing was filled with water, the carpenter's boots were also filled. The water in them was first served out, on account of leakage.

There is a large sound formed here, to which we gave the name of Sandwich's Sound, and commodious anchorage for shipping in the bay, to which we gave the name of Wolf's Bay, in which there is from five to seven fathom water all round. This is extremely well situated for a rendezvous in surveying Endeavour Straits; and were a little colony settled here, a concatenation of Christian settlements would enchain the world, and be useful to any unfortunate ship of whatever nation, that might be wrecked in these seas; or, should a rupture take place in South America, a great vein of commerce might find its way through this channel.

Hammond's Island lies north west and by west, Parker's Island from north and by west to north and by east, and an island seen to the north entrance north west. We supposed it to be an island called by Captain Bligh Mountainous Island, laid down in latitude 10.16 South.

Sandwich's Sound is formed by Hammond's, Parker's, and a cluster of small islands on the starboard hand, at its eastern entrance. We also called a back land behind Hammond's Island, and the other islands to the southward of it, Cornwallis's Land. The uppermost part of the mountain was separated from the main by a large gap. Under the gap, low land was seen; but whether that was a continuation of the main or not, we could not determine. Near the centre of the sound is a small dark-coloured, rocky island.

This afternoon, at three o'clock, being the 2nd of September, our little squadron sailed again, and in the evening saw a high peaked island lying north west, which we called Hawkesbury's Island. The passage through the north entrance is about two miles wide. After passing through it, saw a reef. As we approached it, we shallowed our water to three fathom; but on hauling up more to the south west, we deepened it again to six fathom. Saw several very large turtle, but could not catch any of them. After clearing the reef, stood to the westward. Mountainous Island bore N. half E.; Captain Bligh's west island, which appears in Three Hummocks, N.N.W.; a rock N.W. at the S.W. extreme of the main land, S. and by E.; and the northernmost cape of New South Wales, S.S.E.; and to the extreme of the land in sight, the eastward E. half N. a small distance from the nearest of the Prince of Wales's Islands, we discovered another island, and which we called Christian's Island. Saw Two Hummock between Hawkesbury's Island and Mountainous Island; but could not be certain whether it was one or two islands.

We now entered the great Indian ocean, and had a voyage of a thousand miles to undertake in our open boats. As soon as we cleared the land, we found a very heavy swell running, which threatened destruction to our little fleet; for should we have separated, we must inevitably perish for want of water, as we had not utensils to divide our slender stock. For our mutual preservation, we took each other in tow again; but the sea was so rough, and the swell running so high, we towed very hard, and broke a new tow-line. This put us in the utmost confusion, being afraid of dashing to pieces upon each other, as it was a very dark night. We again made fast to each other; but the tow-line breaking a second time, we were obliged to trust ourselves to the mercy of the waves. At five in the morning, the pinnace lay to, as the other boats had passed her under a dark cloud; but on the signal being made for the boats to join, we again met at daylight. At meridian, we passed some remarkable black and yellow striped sea snakes. On the afternoon of the 4th of September, gave out the exact latitude of our rendezvous in writing; also the longitude by the time-keeper at this present time, in case of unavoidable separation.

On the night between the 5th and 6th, the sea running very cross and high, the tow-line broke several times; the boats strained, and made much water; and we were obliged to leave off towing the rest of the voyage, or it would have dragged the boats asunder. On the 7th, the captain's boat caught a booby. They sucked his blood, and divided him into twenty-four shares.

The men who were employed steering the boats, were often subject to a *coup de soleil*, as every one else were continually wetting their shirts overboard, and putting it upon their head, which alleviated the scorching heat of the sun, to which we were entirely exposed, most of us having lost our hats while swimming at the time the ship was wrecked. It may be observed, that this method of wetting our bodies with salt water is not advisable, if the misery is protracted beyond three or four days, as, after that time, the great absorption from the skin that takes place from the increased heat and fever, makes the fluids become tainted with the bittern of the salt water; so much so, that the saliva became intolerable in the mouth. It may likewise be worthy of remark, that those who drank their own urine died in the sequel of the voyage.

We now neglected weighing our slender allowance of bread, our mouths becoming so parched, that few attempted to eat; and what was not claimed was thrown into the general stock. We found old people suffer much more than those that were young. A particular instance of that we observed in one young boy, a midshipman, who sold his allowance of water two days for one allowance of bread. As their sufferings continued, they became very cross and savage in their temper. In the captain's boat, one of the prisoners took to praying, and they gathered round him with much attention and seeming devotion. But the captain suspecting the purity of his doctrines, and unwilling he should make a monopoly of the business, gave prayers himself. On the 9th, we passed a great many of the Nautilus fish, the shell of which served us to put our glass of water into; by which means we had more time granted to dip our finger in it, and wet our mouths by slow degrees. There were several flocks of birds seen flying in a direction for the land.

On the 13th, in the morning, we saw the land, and the discoverer was immediately rewarded with a glass of water; but, as if our cup of misery was not completely full, it fell a dead calm. The boats now all separated, every one pushing to make the land. Next day we got pretty near it; but there was a prodigious surf running. Two of our men slung a bottle about their necks, jumped overboard, and swam through the surf. They traversed over a good many miles, till a creek intercepted them; when they came down to the beach, and made signs to us of their not having succeeded. We then brought the boat as near the surf as we durst venture, and picked them up. In running along the coast, about twelve o'clock, we had the pleasure to see the red yawl get into a creek. She had hoisted an English jack at her mast-head, that we might observe her in running down the coast. There was a prodigious surf, and many dangerous shoals, between us and the mouth of the creek; we, however, began to share the remains of our water, and about half a bottle came to each man's share, which we dispatched in an instant.

We now gained fresh spirits, and hazarded every thing in gaining our so much wished for haven. It is but justice here to acknowledge how much we were indebted to the intrepidity, courage, and seaman-like behaviour of Mr. Reynolds the master's mate, who fairly beat her over all the reefs, and brought us safe on shore. The crew of the blue yawl, who had been two or three hours landed, assisted in landing our party. A fine spring of water near to the creek afforded us immediate relief. As soon as we had filled our belly, a guard was placed over the prisoners, and we went to sleep for a few hours on the grass.

In the afternoon, a Chinese chief came down the creek in a canoe, attended by some of the natives, to wait upon us. He was a venerable looking old man; we endeavoured to walk down to the water-side, to receive him, and acquaint him with the nature of our distress.

We addressed him in French and in English, neither of which he understood; but misery was so strongly depicted in our countenances, that language was superfluous. The tears trickling down his venerable cheeks convinced us he saw and felt our misfortunes; and silence was eloquence on the subject.

He made us understand by signs, that without fee or reward we should be supplied with horses, and conducted to Coupang, a Dutch East-India settlement, about seventy miles distant, the place of our rendezvous. This we politely declined, as the nature of our duty in the charge of the prisoners would not admit of it. We took leave of him for the present, after receiving promises of refreshment.

Soon after, crowds of the natives came down with fowls, pigs, milk, and bread. Mr. Innes, the surgeon's mate, happened luckily to have some silver in his pocket, to which they applied the touchstone, but would not give us any thing for guineas. However, anchor-buttons answered the purpose, as they gave us provision for a few buttons, which they refused the same number of guineas for; till a hungry dog, one of the carpenter's crew, happening to pick up an officer's jacket, spoiled the market, by giving it, buttons and all, for a pair of fowls, which a few buttons might have purchased.

All hands were busied in roasting the fowls, and boiling the pork; in the evening we made a very hearty supper. While we were regaling ourselves round a large fire, some wild beast gave a roar in the bushes. Some who had been in India before, declared it was the jackal; we therefore, concluded the lion could not be far off. Some were jocularly observing what a glorious supper the lord of the forest would make of us; but others were rather troubled with the dismal thoughts. This gave a gloomy turn to the conversation; and our minds having been previously much engaged with savages and wild beasts, and our bodies worn out through famine and watching, I believe the contagious effects of fear became pretty general. From Bligh's narrative, and others, we had been warned of the danger of landing in any other part of the island of Timor but Coupang, the Dutch settlement, as they were represented hostile and savage.

It is customary with those people, as we afterwards learnt, to do their hard work, such as beating out their rice at night, to avoid the scorching heat of the sun; and the whole village, which was about two miles off, joined in the general song, which every where cheers and accompanies labour. As they had made us great offers for some cartridges of powder, which our duty could not suffer us to part with, we immediately interpreted this song into the war-hoop, and concluded, that they were going to take by force what they could not gain by entreaty. Nature, however, at last worn out, inclined to rest. The first lieutenant and master went on board of the boats, which were at anchor in the middle of the river, for the better security of the prisoners; and, ranging ourselves round, with our feet to the fire, went to sleep.

At dawn of day, the master gave the huntsman's hollow, which some, from being suddenly awaked, thought they were attacked by the Indians. We were all panic struck, and could not get thoroughly awaked, being so exhausted, and overpowered with sleep. Most of us were scrambling upon all fours down to the river, and crying for Christ's sake to have mercy upon them, till those who were foremost in the scramble, in crawling into the creek, got recovered from their plight by their hands being immersed in water; yet those who were foremost in running away, were not last in upbraiding the rest with cowardice, notwithstanding there were pretty evident marks upon some of them, of the cold water having produced its usual effects of micturition.

Next day we went up the creek, in one of the boats, about four miles, to one of their towns, with an intention of purchasing provisions for our sea-store. As we entered the town, the king was riding out, attended by twenty carabineers or body-guards, well mounted, and respectably armed. He passed us with all the *sang froid* imaginable, scarce deigning to glance at us.

In purchasing a pig, the man finding a good price for it, offered to traffic with us for the charms of his daughter, a very pretty young girl. But none of us seemed inclined that way, as there were many good things we stood much more in need of.

At one o'clock, being high water, we embarked again in our boats for Coupang. We sailed along the coast all day till it was dark; and, fearful lest we should over-shoot our port in the night, put into a bay. After laying some time, we observed a light; and after hallooing and making a noise, the natives came down with torches in their hands, waded up alongside of us, and offered their assistance, which we accepted of, in lighting fires, and dressing the victuals we had brought with us, that no time might be lost in landing or cooking the next day.

At day break, we again proceeded on our voyage, and at five in the afternoon we landed at Coupang. The Governor, Mynheer Vanion, received us with the utmost politeness, kindness, and hospitality. The lieutenant-governor, Mynheer Fry, was likewise extremely kind and attentive, in rendering every assistance possible, and in giving the necessary orders for our support and relief in our present distressed state.

Next morning being Sunday, as we supposed, the 17th of September, we were preparing for Church, to return thanks to Almighty God, for his divine interposition in our miraculous preservation; but were disappointed in our pious intentions; for we found it was Monday, the 18th, having lost a day by performing a circuit of the globe to the westward.

CHAPTER 5

Coupang, Batavia & England

This is the Montpelier of the East to the Dutch and Portuguese settlements in India; and, from the salubrity of its air, is the favourite resort of valetudinarians and invalids from Batavia and other places. This island is fertile, variegated with hill and dale, and equally beautiful as diversified with Rotti, and its appendant isles. It is as large as the island of Great Britain. Its principal trade is wax, honey, and sandalwood; but the whole of its revenues do not defray the expense of the settlement to the company; but from the locality of its situation, it is convenient for their other islands. They had the monopoly of the sandalwood trade, which is used in all temples, mosques, and places of worship in the East, every Chinese having a sprig of it burning day and night near their household-gods.

The exclusive trade of sandalwood was valuable and convenient to the Dutch; but, from the vast extent of territory lately acquired in India, we have plenty of that commodity without going to the Dutch market. Close to the Dutch town is a Chinese town and temple. They have a governor of their own nation, but pay large tribute to the Dutch. Notwithstanding their trade is under very severe restrictions, they soon make rich; and, as soon as they become independent, return to their own country. For European and India goods the natives barter their produce, and sell their prisoners of war, who are carried to Batavia as slaves, and the natives of Java sent from Batavia to this place in return. As they hold their tenure more from policy than strength, it would be impolitic to irritate them, by exposing their countrymen, subjugated to the lash of slavery and oppression.

An instance of this soul-couping business fell under our inspection while here. One of the petty princes, in settling his account with a merchant of this place, was some dollars short of cash. He just stepped to the door, and casting his eye on an elderly man who was near him, he laid hold of him; and, with the assistance of some of his myrmidons, gave him up as a slave, and so settled his account. We felt more interested in the fate of this poor wretch, on account of his having been a prince himself, but never before saw the face of his oppressor. He went passenger in the ship with us to Batavia.

It was a pleasing and flattering sight to an Englishman, at this remotest corner of the globe, to see that Wedgewood's stoneware, and Birmingham goods, had found their way into the shops of Coupang.

During our five weeks stay here, the Governor, Mynheer Vanion, by every act of politeness and attention endeavoured to make us spend our time agreeably. We were sumptuously regaled at his table every day, and the evening was spent with cards and concerts. I could dwell with pleasure for an age in praise of this honest Dutchman; it is the tribute of a grateful heart, and his due. This is the third time he has had an opportunity of extending his hospitality to shipwrecked Englishmen.

About a fortnight before we arrived, a boat, with eight men, a woman, and two children, came on shore here, who told him they were the supercargo, part of the crew, and passengers of an English brig, wrecked in these seas. His house, which has ever been the asylum of the distressed, was open for their reception. They drew bills on the British government, and were supplied with every necessary they stood in need of.

The captain of a Dutch East Indiaman, who spoke English, hearing of the arrival of Captain Edwards, and our unfortunate boat, run to them with the glad tidings of their captain having arrived; but one of them, starting up in surprise, said, "What captain! Damn me, we have no captain;" for they had reported, that the captain and remainder of the crew had separated from them at sea in another boat. This immediately led to a suspicion of their being impostors; and they were ordered to be apprehended, and put into the castle. One of the men, and the woman, fled into the woods; but were soon taken. They confessed they were English convicts, and that they had made their escape from Botany Bay. They had been supplied with a quadrant, a compass, a chart, and some small arms and ammunition, from a Dutch ship that lay there; and the expedition was conducted by the governor's fisherman, whose time of transportation was expired. He was a good seaman, and a tolerable navigator. They dragged along the coast of New South Wales; and as often as the hostile nature of the savage natives would permit, hauled their boat up at night, and slept on shore. They met with several curious and interesting anecdotes in this voyage. In many places of the coast of South Wales, they found very good coal; a circumstance that was not before known. Our men were now beginning to regain their strength; and Captain Dadleberg of the *Rembang* Indiaman was making every possible dispatch with his ship to carry us to Batavia.

During this time, the interment of Balthazar, King of Coupang, was performed with much funeral pomp. The governor, lieutenant-governor, and all the Europeans were invited. Six months had been spent in preparations for this fête, at which an emperor and twenty-five kings assisted and attended in person with all their body-guards, standards, and standard-bearers, were present. When the corpse was deposited in the sepulchre, the company's troops fired three volleys, and victuals and drink were immediately served to four thousand people.

The Dutch and English officers were invited to a very sumptuous dinner, at a table provided for the emperor and all the kings. The first toast after dinner was the dead king's health. Next they drank Mynheer Company's health, which was accompanied with a volley of small arms and *paterreros*. The singularity of Mynheer Company's health, led us to request an explanation; when we were informed, they found it necessary to make them believe that Mynheer Company was a great and powerful king, lest they should not be inclined to pay that submission to a company of merchants.

The inaugural ceremony at the installation of the young king, was performed by his drinking a bumper of brandy and gunpowder, stirred round with the point of a sword. After being invested with the regal dignity, he came down in state, to pay his respects to the governor. As he was preceded by music, and colours flying, every one turned out to see him. Amongst the rest was a captive king in chains, who was employed blowing the bellows to our armourer, whilst he was forging bolts and fetters for our prisoners and convicts. Here the sunshine of prosperity, and the mutability of human greatness, were excellently portrayed.

By a policy in the Dutch, in supplying the petty princes with ammunition and warlike stores, feuds and dissentions are kindled amongst them; and they are kept so completely engaged in civil war, that they have no time to observe the encroachments of strangers. That domestic strife serves likewise amply to supply the slave trade from the prisoners of both parties. They, however, some time since, made head against the common enemy, and forced the Dutch to retire within their trenches.

It is the custom, in this climate, to bathe morning and evening. A fine river, which runs in the centre of the town, is conveniently situated for that purpose; and we availed ourselves of it when our strength would permit. Nature has been profusely lavish, in producing, in the neighbourhood of this place, all the varied powers of landscape that the most luxuriant fancy can suggest. But, while enjoying the picturesque beauties of the scene, or sheltering in the translucent stream from the fervour of meridian heat, you are suddenly chilled with fear, from the terrific aspect of the alligator, or crested snake, and a number of venomous reptiles, with which this country abounds. There is one in particular called the *cowk cowk*; it is the most disgusting looking animal that creeps the ground, and its bite is mortal. It is about a foot and a half long, and seems a production between the toad and lizard. At stated periods it makes a noise exactly like a cuckoo clock. Even the natives fly from it with the utmost horror. The alligators are daring and numerous. There are instances of their devouring men and children when bathing in the shallow part of the river above the town.

The Governor, Mynheer Vanion, relates a circumstance that happened to him while hunting. In crossing a shallow part of the river, his black boy was snapped up by an alligator; but the Governor immediately dismounted, rescued the boy out of his mouth, and slew him.

The natives of Timor are subject to a *cutaneous* disease during their infancy, something similar to the small pox, but of longer duration. It seldom terminates fatally, and only seizes them once in their lives.[1]

On the 6th of October, we embarked on board the *Rembang* Dutch Indiaman, taking with us the prisoners and convicts. Our crew became very sickly in passing the Straits of Alice. We had frequent calms and sultry weather until the 12th. In passing the island of Flores, a most tremendous storm arose. In a few minutes every sail of the ship was shivered to pieces; the pumps all choked, and useless; the leak gaining fast upon us; and she was driving down, with all the impetuosity imaginable, on a savage shore, about seven miles under our lee. This storm was attended with the most dreadful thunder and lightning we had ever experienced. The Dutch seamen were struck with horror, and went below; and the ship was preserved from destruction by the manly exertion of our English tars, whose souls seemed to catch redoubled ardour from the tempest's rage. Indeed it is only in these trying moments of distress, when the abyss of destruction is yawning to receive them, that the transcendent worth of a British seaman is most conspicuous. Nor would I wish, from what I have observed above, to throw any stigma on the Dutch, who I believe would fight the devil, should he appear in any other shape to them but that of thunder and lightning.

It may be remarked, that the Straits of Alice are not so dan-

---

1. This seems to be the earliest description of Yaws (*Framboesia*) in these islands. Originating in Africa this contagious disease is believed to have been disseminated by the slave trade. The Dutch or Portuguese traders carried it from Madagascar and East Africa to Ceylon, where it still bears the name of *Parangi Lede*, or Foreigners' Evil. Though Hamilton did not observe it in the South Sea Islands the disease was probably there, for Mariner, who was in Tonga in 1810, described it as a well-established disease under the name of *Tona*.

gerous as those of Sapy, and are for many reasons preferable; but it is so intricate a navigation that a Dutchman bound from Timor to Batavia, after beating about for twelve months, found himself exactly where he first started from.

On the 21st, we got through Alice, and saw three prow-vessels, who are a very daring set of pirates that infest those seas. On the 22nd, saw the islands of Kangajunk and Ulk, and run through the channel that is between them. Next day we saw the island of Madura.

On the 26th, saw the island of Java; and on the 30th, anchored at Samarang.

Immediately on our coming to anchor, we were agreeably surprised to find our tender here which we had so long given up for lost. Never was social affection more eminently portrayed than in the meeting of these poor fellows; and from excess of joy, and a recital of their mutual sufferings, from pestilence, famine, and shipwreck, a flood of tears filled every man's breast.

They informed us, the night they parted company with us, the savages attacked them in a regular and powerful body in their canoes; and their never having seen a European ship before, nor being able to conceive any idea of fire-arms, made the conflict last longer than it otherwise would; for, seeing no missive weapon made use of, when their companions were killed, they did not suspect any thing to be the matter with them, as they tumbled into the water. Our seven-barrelled pieces made great havoc amongst them. One fellow had agility enough to spring over their boarding-netting, and was levelling a blow with his war-club at Mr. Oliver, the commanding-officer, who had the good fortune to shoot him.

On not finding the ship next day, they gave up all further hopes of her, and steered for Anamooka, the rendezvous Captain Edwards had appointed. Their distress for want of water, if possible, surpassed that of our own, and had so strong an effect on one of the young gentlemen, that the day following he became delirious, and continued so for some months after it.

They at last made the island of Tofoa, near to Anamooka, which they mistook for it. After trading with the natives for provisions and water, they made an attempt to take the vessel from them, which they always will to a small vessel, when alone; but they were soon overpowered with the fire arms. They were, however, obliged to be much on their guard afterwards, at those islands which were inhabited.

After much diversity of distress, and similar encounters, they at last made the reef that runs between New Guinea and New Holland, where the *Pandora* met her unhappy fate; and after traversing from shore to shore, without finding an opening, this intrepid young seaman boldly gave it the stem, and beat over the reef. The alternative was dreadful, as famine presented them on the one hand, and shipwreck on the other. Soon after they had passed Endeavour Straits, they fell in with a small Dutch vessel, who showed them every tenderness that the nature of their distress required.

They were soon landed at a small Dutch settlement; but the governor having a description of the *Bounty*'s pirates from our court, and their vessel being built of foreign timber, served to confirm them in their suspicions; and as no officer in the British navy bears a commission or warrant under the rank of lieutenant, where, by seal of office, their person or quality may be identified, they had only their bare *ipse dixit* to depend on. They, however, behaved to them with great precaution and humanity. Although they kept a strict guard over them, nothing was withheld to render their situation agreeable; and they were sent, under a proper escort, to this place.

This settlement is reckoned next to Batavia, and is so lucrative, that the governor is changed every five years. The present governor's name is Overstraaten, a gentleman of splendid taste and unbounded hospitality, who lives in a princely style; and to the *otium dignitate* of Asiatic luxury, has the happiness to join an honest hearty Dutch welcome.

A regiment of the Duke of Württemberg is doing duty here, amongst whom were several men of rank and fashion, who showed us much civility and politeness.

The town is regular and beautiful, and the houses are built in a style of architecture, which has given loose to the most sportive fancy. Each street is terminated with some public building, such as a great marine school, for the education of young officers and seamen; an hospital for decayed officers in the company's service; churches; the governor's palace, &c. &c. Here the *utile dulce* has not been neglected, and those objects of national importance are placed in a proper point of view, as the just pride and ornament of a great commercial people.

Such is the effect of early prejudices, that, under the muzzle of the sun, a Dutchman cannot exist without snuffing the putrid exhalations from stagnant water, to which they have been accustomed from their infancy. They are intersecting it so fast with canals, that in a year or two this beautiful town will be completely dammed.

In a few days, we arrived at Batavia, the emporium of the Dutch in the east; and our first care was employed in sending to the hospital the sickly remains of our unfortunate crew. Some dead bodies floating down the canal struck our boat, which had a very disagreeable effect on the minds of our brave fellows, whose nerves were reduced to a very weak state from sickness. This was a *coup de grace* to a sick man on his *premier entree* into this painted sepulchre, this Golgotha of Europe, which buries the whole settlement every five years.

It is not the climate I am inveighing against; it is the Gothic, diabolical ideas of the people I indite.

Were they only Dutchmen who supplied the ravenous maw of death, it would be impertinence in me to make any comment on it; but when the whole globe lends its aid to supply this destructive settlement, and its baneful effects arising more from the letch a Dutchman has for stagnant mud than from climate, I hope the indulgent reader will pardon my spleen, when I tell them professionally that all the mortality of that place originates from marsh effluvia, arising from their stagnant canals and pleasure-grounds.

The Chinese are here the Jews of the East, and as soon as they make their fortune, they go home. Let the amateurs of the Republican system read and learn. Be not surprised when it is observed, that these little great men, those vile hawkers of spice and nutmegs, exact a submission that the most absolute and tyrannical monarch who ever swayed a sceptre would be ashamed of. The compass of my work will not allow me to be particular; but I must instance one among many others. When an *edilleer*, or one of the supreme council, meets a carriage, the gentleman who meets him must alight, and make him a perfect bow in spirit; not one of Bunburry's long bows, but that bow which carries humility and submission in it, that sort of bow which every vertebra in an English back is *anchylosed* against.

In our passage from this to the Cape, before we left Java, one of the convicts had jumped over board in the night, and swam to the Dutch arsenal at Honroost. In passing Bantan, we viewed the relics of Lord Cathcart. We met nothing particular in passing the island of Sumatra, but experienced great death and sickness in going through the Straits of Sunda; and after a tedious passage, arrived at the Cape of Good Hope.

Here we met with many civilities from Colonel Gordon; a gentleman no less eminent for his private virtues than his extraordinary military and literary accomplishments. From his labours, all the host of voyagers and historians of that part of the globe have been purloining; but it is to be hoped the world will, at some future period, be favoured with his works unmutilated.

The town is gay, and from length of habit, the inhabitants partake much of the manners of Bath; and, for a short season, behave with the utmost attention and tenderness. Their dress and customs are more characteristic of the English than Dutch. An uncommon rage for building has lately prevailed; and although they cannot boast of that chastity of style in which Samarang is built it is gaudy, and calculated to please the generality of observers.

Allow me to mention the singular manner in which the monkeys make depredations on the gardens here. They place a proper piquet, or advanced guard, as sentinels, when a party is drawn up in a line, who hand the fruit from one to another; and when the alarm is given by the piquet-guard, they all take flight, making sure that by that time the booty is conveyed to a considerable distance. But should the piquet be negligent in their duty, and suffer the main body to be surprised, the delinquents are severely punished.

The same ill-fated rage for canalling-murder prevails here. They have even contrived to carry canals to the top of a mountain. The boors, or country-farmers, are a species of the human race, so gigantic and superior to the rest of mankind, in point of size and constitution, that they may be called nondescripts.

Their hospital, as to site, surpasses any in the world. It may be observed, however, that the architect, by the smallness of the windows, which only serve to exclude the light and air, seems to have studied, with much ingenuity, to render it a cadaverous stinking prison.

After being refreshed at the Cape, we passed St. Helena, the island of Ascension, and arrived at Holland; and had the happiness, through the interposition of divine Providence, to be again landed on our native shore.

THE LATITUDES AND LONGITUDES OF THE DIFFERENT PLACES TOUCHED AT OR DISCOVERED BY HIS MAJESTY'S SHIP *PANDORA*, TAKEN WITH THE GREATEST ACCURACY FROM THE CENTRE OF THE ISLANDS

Names of Places.	Latitudes.			Longitudes.			
Gomera, - - - - -	28	5	N	17	8		W
Canary, N.E. point, - - -	28	13	N	15	38		W
Teneriffe, Santa Cruz, - -	28	27	N	16	16		W
Palma, - - - - -	28	36	N	17	45		W
St. Antonio, Cape de Verd Islands,							
crossing the Line, - - -	17	0	N	25	2		W
Rio Janeiro, - - - -	22	54	S				
Patagonia, Straits of Magellan,							
Cape Julian, Staten Island, -	54	47	30 S	63	58	27	W
Cape Horn, - - - -	55	59	S	67	21		W
Diego Ramarez, - - -							
Easter Island, - - - -	27	7	S	109	42		W
Ducie's Island, - - - -	24	40	30 S	124	40	30	W
Lord Hood's Island, - - -	21	31	S	135	32	30	W
Carysfort Island, - - -	20	49	S	138	33		W
Maitea, - - - - -	17	52	S	148	6		W
Otaheite, Matavy Bay, - -	17	29	S	149	35		W
Huaheine, Owharre Bay, - -	16	44	S	151	3		W
Ulitea and Otaha, - - -	16	46	S	151	33		W
Bolobola, - - - -	16	33	S	151	52		W
Mauruah, - - - -	16	26	S	152	33		W
Whytutakee, - - - -	18	52	S	159	41		W
Palmerston's Isles, - - -	18	0	S	162	57		W
Duke of York's Island, - -	8	33	30 S	172	4	3	W
Duke of Clarence's Island, - -	9	9	30 S	171	30	46	W
Chatham's Island, - - -	13	32	20 S	172	18	20	W
Ohatooah, - - - -	13	50	S	171	30	6	W
Anamooka, - - - -	20	16	S	174	30		W

Names of Places.		Latitudes.	Longitudes.
Toomanuah, - - - -		14 15 S	169 43 W
Otutuelah, - - - -		14 30 S	170 41 W
Howe's Island, - - - -		18 32 30 S	173 53 W
Bickerton's Island, - - -		18 47 40 S	174 48 W
Gardner's Island, - - -		17 57 S	175 16 54 W
Pylestaart, - - - -		22 23 S	175 39 W
Eoah or Middleburgh, - -		21 21 S	174 34 W
Tongataboo, - - - -		21 9 S	174 41 W
Proby's Island, - - -		15 53 S	175 51 W
Wallis's Island, - - -		13 22 S	176 15 45 W
Grenville Island, - - -		12 29 S	183 3 } W 176 57 } E
Pandora's Reef, - - -		12 11 S	188 8 } W 171 52 } E
Mitre Island, - - - -		11 49 S	190 4 30 } W 169 55 30 } E
Cherry Island, - - - -		11 37 30 S	190 19 30 } W 169 55 30 } E
Pitt's Island, - - - -		11 50 30 S	193 14 15 } W 166 45 45 } E
Wells's Shoal, - - - -		12 20 S	202 2 } W 157 58 } E
Cape Rodney, } Point of M. Clarence in shore, } New Guinea		10 3 32 S	212 14 5 } W 147 45 45 } E
Cape Hood, }		9 58 6 S	212 37 10 } W 147 22 50 } E
Murray's Isles, - - -		9 57 S	216 43 } W 143 17 } E
Wreck Reef, - - - -		11 22 S	216 22 } W 143 38 } E
Batavia, - - - -		6 10 S	106 51 E
Straits of Sunda, - - -		6 36 15 S	105 17 30 E
Cape of Good Hope, - - -		34 29 S	18 23 E
St. Helena, - - - -		15 55 S	5 49 W
Ascension Island, - - -		7 56 S	14 32 W

LEONAUR

ALSO FROM LEONAUR
AVAILABLE IN SOFTCOVER OR HARDCOVER WITH DUST JACKET

CAPTAIN OF THE 95th (Rifles) *by Jonathan Leach*—An officer of Wellington's Sharpshooters during the Peninsular, South of France and Waterloo Campaigns of the Napoleonic Wars.

BUGLER AND OFFICER OF THE RIFLES *by William Green & Harry Smith* With the 95th (Rifles) during the Peninsular & Waterloo Campaigns of the Napoleonic Wars

BAYONETS, BUGLES AND BONNETS by *James 'Thomas' Todd*—Experiences of hard soldiering with the 71st Foot - the Highland Light Infantry - through many battles of the Napoleonic wars including the Peninsular & Waterloo Campaigns

THE ADVENTURES OF A LIGHT DRAGOON *by George Farmer & G.R. Gleig*—A cavalryman during the Peninsular & Waterloo Campaigns, in captivity & at the siege of Bhurtpore, India

THE COMPLEAT RIFLEMAN HARRIS *by Benjamin Harris as told to & transcribed by Captain Henry Curling*—The adventures of a soldier of the 95th (Rifles) during the Peninsular Campaign of the Napoleonic Wars

WITH WELLINGTON'S LIGHT CAVALRY *by William Tomkinson*—The Experiences of an officer of the 16th Light Dragoons in the Peninsular and Waterloo campaigns of the Napoleonic Wars.

SURTEES OF THE RIFLES by *William Surtees*—A Soldier of the 95th (Rifles) in the Peninsular campaign of the Napoleonic Wars.

ENSIGN BELL IN THE PENINSULAR WAR *by George Bell*—The Experiences of a young British Soldier of the 34th Regiment 'The Cumberland Gentlemen' in the Napoleonic wars.

WITH THE LIGHT DIVISION by *John H. Cooke*—The Experiences of an Officer of the 43rd Light Infantry in the Peninsula and South of France During the Napoleonic Wars

NAPOLEON'S IMPERIAL GUARD: FROM MARENGO TO WATERLOO by *J. T. Headley*—This is the story of Napoleon's Imperial Guard from the bearskin caps of the grenadiers to the flamboyance of their mounted chasseurs, their principal characters and the men who commanded them.

BATTLES & SIEGES OF THE PENINSULAR WAR by *W. H. Fitchett*—Corunna, Busaco, Albuera, Ciudad Rodrigo, Badajos, Salamanca, San Sebastian & Others

LEONAUR

ALSO FROM LEONAUR

AVAILABLE IN SOFTCOVER OR HARDCOVER WITH DUST JACKET

WELLINGTON AND THE PYRENEES CAMPAIGN VOLUME I: FROM VITORIA TO THE BIDASSOA by F. C. Beatson—The final phase of the campaign in the Iberian Peninsula.

WELLINGTON AND THE INVASION OF FRANCE VOLUME II: THE BIDASSOA TO THE BATTLE OF THE NIVELLE by F. C. Beatson—The second of Beatson's series on the fall of Revolutionary France published by Leonaur, the reader is once again taken into the centre of Wellington's strategic and tactical genius.

WELLINGTON AND THE FALL OF FRANCE VOLUME III: THE GAVES AND THE BATTLE OF ORTHEZ by F. C. Beatson—This final chapter of F. C. Beatson's brilliant trilogy shows the 'captain of the age' at his most inspired and makes all three books essential additions to any Peninsular War library.

NAVAL BATTLES OF THE NAPOLEONIC WARS by W. H. Fitchett—Cape St.Vincent, the Nile, Cadiz, Copenhagen, Trafalgar & Others

SERGEANT GUILLEMARD: THE MAN WHO SHOT NELSON? by Robert Guillemard—A Soldier of the Infantry of the French Army of Napoleon on Campaign Throughout Europe

WITH THE GUARDS ACROSS THE PYRENEES by Robert Batty—The Experiences of a British Officer of Wellington's Army During the Battles for the Fall of Napoleonic France, 1813.

A STAFF OFFICER IN THE PENINSULA by E. W. Buckham—An Officer of the British Staff Corps Cavalry During the Peninsula Campaign of the Napoleonic Wars

THE LEIPZIG CAMPAIGN: 1813—NAPOLEON AND THE "BATTLE OF THE NATIONS" by F. N. Maude—Colonel Maude's analysis of Napoleon's campaign of 1813.

BUGEAUD: A PACK WITH A BATON by Thomas Robert Bugeaud—The Early Campaigns of a Soldier of Napoleon's Army Who Would Become a Marshal of France.

TWO LEONAUR ORIGINALS

SERGEANT NICOL by Daniel Nicol—The Experiences of a Gordon Highlander During the Napoleonic Wars in Egypt, the Peninsula and France.

WATERLOO RECOLLECTIONS by Frederick Llewellyn—Rare First Hand Accounts, Letters, Reports and Retellings from the Campaign of 1815.

LEONAUR

ALSO FROM LEONAUR
AVAILABLE IN SOFTCOVER OR HARDCOVER WITH DUST JACKET

THE JENA CAMPAIGN: 1806 *by F. N. Maude*—The Twin Battles of Jena & Auerstadt Between Napoleon's French and the Prussian Army.

PRIVATE O'NEIL *by Charles O'Neil*—The recollections of an Irish Rogue of H. M. 28th Regt.—The Slashers— during the Peninsula & Waterloo campaigns of the Napoleonic wars.

ROYAL HIGHLANDER *by James Anton*—A soldier of H.M 42nd (Royal) Highlanders during the Peninsular, South of France & Waterloo Campaigns of the Napoleonic Wars.

CAPTAIN BLAZE *by Elzéar Blaze*—Elzéar Blaze recounts his life and experiences in Napoleon's army in a well written, articulate and companionable style.

LEJEUNE VOLUME 1 *by Louis-François Lejeune*—The Napoleonic Wars through the Experiences of an Officer on Berthier's Staff.

LEJEUNE VOLUME 2 *by Louis-François Lejeune*—The Napoleonic Wars through the Experiences of an Officer on Berthier's Staff.

FUSILIER COOPER *by John S. Cooper*—Experiences in the 7th (Royal) Fusiliers During the Peninsular Campaign of the Napoleonic Wars and the American Campaign to New Orleans.

CAPTAIN COIGNET *by Jean-Roch Coignet*—A Soldier of Napoleon's Imperial Guard from the Italian Campaign to Russia and Waterloo.

FIGHTING NAPOLEON'S EMPIRE *by Joseph Anderson*—The Campaigns of a British Infantryman in Italy, Egypt, the Peninsular & the West Indies During the Napoleonic Wars.

CHASSEUR BARRES *by Jean-Baptiste Barres*—The experiences of a French Infantryman of the Imperial Guard at Austerlitz, Jena, Eylau, Friedland, in the Peninsular, Lutzen, Bautzen, Zinnwald and Hanau during the Napoleonic Wars.

MARINES TO 95TH (RIFLES) *by Thomas Fernyhough*—The military experiences of Robert Fernyhough during the Napoleonic Wars.

HUSSAR ROCCA *by Albert Jean Michel de Rocca*—A French cavalry officer's experiences of the Napoleonic Wars and his views on the Peninsular Campaigns against the Spanish, British And Guerilla Armies.

SERGEANT BOURGOGNE *by Adrien Bourgogne*—With Napoleon's Imperial Guard in the Russian Campaign and on the Retreat from Moscow 1812 - 13.

9 781846 776014